THE
GOVERNMENT OF EDEN

Spiritual Principles for Living in Peace

Writings by Joel S. Goldsmith

A Message for the Ages

A Parenthesis in Eternity

Awakening Mystical Consciousness

Beyond Words and Thoughts

Collected Essays

Conscious Union with God

Consciousness in Transition

Consciousness Is What I Am

Consciousness Transformed

Consciousness Unfolding

God Formed Us for His Glory

God, the Substance of All Form

I Stand on Holy Ground

Invisible Supply

Leave Your Nets

Living Between Two Worlds

Living by Grace

Living by the Word

Living Now

Living the Illumined Life

Living the Infinite Way

Man Was Not Born to Cry

Our Spiritual Resources

Practicing the Presence

Realization of Oneness

Rising in Consciousness

Seek Ye First

Showing Forth the Presence of God

Spiritual Discernment

Spiritual Interpretation of Scripture

Spiritual Power of Truth

The Altitude of Prayer

The Art of Meditation

The Art of Spiritual Healing

The Art of Spiritual Living

The Christmas Letters

The Contemplative Life

The Early Years

The Easter Letters

The Foundation of Mysticism

The Gift of Love

The Heart of Mysticism: Vols. I–VI

The Infinite Way

The Joel Goldsmith Reader

The Journey Back to the Father's House

The Master Speaks

The Mystical I

The Only Freedom

The Thunder of Silence

The World Is New

All titles listed above can be found at www.AcropolisBooks.com.

THE
GOVERNMENT OF EDEN

Spiritual Principles for Living in Peace

Joel S. Goldsmith

Compiled and Edited
by Acropolis Books

Acropolis Books, Publisher
Longboat Key, Florida

THE GOVERNMENT OF EDEN
SPIRITUAL PRINCIPLES FOR LIVING IN PEACE

Copyright © 2020 by Acropolis Books, Inc.

ISBN 978-0-87491-001-8

All Bible quotations are taken from THE KING JAMES VERSION

Published by Acropolis Books.

For information contact:
Acropolis Books, Inc.
Longboat Key, Florida

http://www.acropolisbooks.com

Book design by Palomar Print Design

Cover image: "The Garden of Eden" by Thomas Cole (1828)

Goldsmith, Joel S.,   1892—1964.
  The garden of eden: spiritual principles for living in peace / Joel S.
Goldsmith; edited by Acropolis Books.

Except the Lord build the house,
they labour in vain that build it.

Psalm 127

"Illumination dissolves all material ties and binds men together with the golden chains of spiritual understanding; it acknowledges only the leadership of the Christ; it has no ritual or rule but the divine, impersonal universal Love; no other worship than the inner Flame that is ever lit at the shrine of Spirit. This union is the free state of spiritual brotherhood. The only restraint is the discipline of Soul; therefore, we know liberty without license; we are a united universe without physical limits; a divine service to God without ceremony or creed. The illumined walk without fear — by Grace."

From *The Infinite Way*
by Joel S. Goldsmith

CONTENTS

CONTENTS

PART 4
RETURN TO THE GARDEN OF EDEN

Publisher's Preface

THE MISSION OF Acropolis Books has been to ensure that the complete written works of Joel S. Goldsmith are preserved and accessible for generations to come. To that end, all of Joel's books are now available in both electronic and print formats, and a number of these titles have been published in foreign languages as well. Acropolis has also been granted permission to upgrade the consistency of the transcripts of Joel's recorded lectures for professional publication, which total over 1,300 hours of audio. Since the content of Joel's current books has been drawn from only about a third of his audio recordings, there remains a vast amount of new material to be published on the topics of spiritual living and practical mysticism.

To complement the study of Joel's books and transcripts, the Acropolis website provides an online utility to search his entire library of works for any word, phrase, or subject of interest. This invaluable resource enables the student as well as the publisher to concentrate on a particular theme that Joel has addressed in numerous places throughout his years of teaching. *The Government of Eden* is the result of this focused approach as facilitated by modern digital technology. The content of this book was compiled by meticulously selecting and integrating relevant material in Joel's own words from hundreds of transcripts and previously published works to create a coherent sequence of chapters for enhanced readability and comprehension. The excerpts comprising each chapter of the book are listed in the appendix for easy reference.

Acropolis Books is deeply grateful to the Estate of Joel S. Goldsmith for the privilege of publishing his profound spiritual teachings that continue to bless the many and glorify the One.

Publisher's notes:

Throughout this book, in-line Bible verses and quotations attributed to individuals may represent the essence of the verse or statement or may be an exact quotation. Footnotes provide the appropriate reference.

In the spiritual literature of the world, the varying concepts of God are indicated by the use of such words as "Father," "Mother," "Soul," "Spirit," "Principle," "Love," "Life." Therefore, in this book the author has used the pronouns "I," "Me," "He," "It," "Himself," and "Itself," interchangeably in referring to God.

During the 1950s and '60s, masculine pronouns were commonly used to refer to God and to individuals or groups of any gender. Today such gender bias is disappearing. While Acropolis Books supports gender inclusivity in spiritual literature, the editors have chosen not to alter the masculine pronouns in this book in order to present Joel's teaching as it was originally expressed.

Introduction

HISTORY SHOWS THAT the twentieth century was a time of both national and international upheaval marked by grave military, political, and social conflict of far-reaching consequences. While governments around the globe struggled at great cost with these overwhelming challenges, a few spiritually-illuminated men and women turned to a means of peaceful resolution, not on the level of strife, but on the level of grace and truth. One such enlightened individual was Joel Goldsmith: the mystic, healer, and teacher who traveled the world in the 1950s and 1960s revealing spiritual principles that he found to be practical and effective not only in political and social arenas, but also in the areas of health, relationships, finances, and business. Joel was not imparting theory, philosophy, or dogma, but divine laws proven to be universal and eternal, for the crises of his day were not unique to one generation or to one country. The issues facing the world in the twentieth century existed for eons and continue to confront us in the present age because, as Joel discovered, these are not problems in time and space, but discords in human consciousness.

Joel never denied the difficulties of human existence, nor did he ignore the responsibilities of family life, career, or citizenship. He demonstrated a direct and successful way of dealing with our mortal challenges while fulfilling our secular obligations. Without overreacting to headlines, emergency calls, or personal commitments, Joel dealt with one demand after another—spiritually. Contrary to humanity's efforts to survive by force, Joel revealed a means to thrive by grace. This was a path to true freedom and lasting peace that was critically dependent on its starting point, which for Joel was always God. This God, however, was not a deity awaiting us in the hereafter. Nor was this God a supreme genie granting our prayerful wishes. Joel's constant and consistent starting point was the God of individual consciousness, and he often referred to this high state of spiritual consciousness as the Garden of Eden. This is the divine realm within each and every one of us that Jesus called the kingdom of God, where the government is upon His shoulders.

In this Edenic state of consciousness, we are peacefully yet firmly ruled by Spirit in all matters of our daily living, and "where the Spirit of the Lord is, there is liberty:"[1] liberty from fear, anxiety, anger, insecurity, and doubt. If we are to follow the clear and fruitful truth teachings of our way-showers, such as Jesus and Joel, then we too must begin our every task by seeking the guidance of the divine Presence that governs us by grace from the inside out. In this way, the harmony of individual consciousness brings an ever-greater peace to our world as illustrated in *The Government of Eden*.

This latest compilation of excerpts from Joel Goldsmith's many lectures presents an enlightening message of assurance, conviction, and practicality that is both timely and timeless. *The Government of Eden* is an extraordinary collection of Joel's teachings that focus sharply on the nature of our divine consciousness and on our responsibilities as spiritual citizens in the here-and-now. In this remarkable book, with clarity and authority, Joel details a spiritual approach to national and international affairs, governing, voting, politics, equality, tolerance, and other crucial issues that confront us on a regular basis. Throughout this work, Joel is not only calling us back to the peaceful garden of freedom and fulfillment within, but also guiding us to and through the gates of Eden, which have never been locked —except in belief. *The Government of Eden*, however, dispels that erroneous belief with the truth that sets us free in the face of every worldly challenge.

An Invitation

ONLY THE VERY courageous can embark on the spiritual journey, and only those of great strength and vision can hope to continue on this path. Nearly twenty centuries ago, the Master made it clear that "the way is strait and narrow and few there be that enter."[1] That this is true is borne out by the fact that, up to the present time, very few have been able to remain on the spiritual path and continue to go forward. It is not easy to surmount superstition, ignorance, and fear, and, despite prejudice and previous failures, to set forth in search of new horizons.

We cannot adopt new ideas while still clinging to the outworn beliefs of the past: we must be willing to relinquish our old concepts. That is where the courage comes in, and the daring.

Every year will be the result of what we make of it, the result of something that we put into operation this minute. It will not do to wait until midnight tonight; it will not do to wait until tomorrow. The kind of year that we are to experience must be started now, in this moment, by an act of decision, and each one must make that decision for himself.

Joel S. Goldsmith

PART 1

THE COURAGEOUS CHOICE

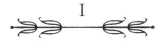

GOVERNED BY GOD OR GOVERNED BY MAN?

EVERY FOUR YEARS, as attention in the United States is focused upon the selection of the President and Vice President of the United States, Infinite Way students are reminded of how important it is to realize that "the government is on His shoulders."[1] The "ten righteous men,"[2] those who know this truth, can play a significant role in bringing to pass God's government on earth as it is in heaven.

An election is an opportunity for citizens to exercise the franchise and vote for the candidates of their choice. To vote intelligently and fulfill his responsibility as a citizen, every voter should be thoroughly familiar with the issues and know how each candidate stands on these issues, not only in terms of what he says but in terms of his record. It is the responsibility of an informed citizenry, and Infinite Way students should fall into that category.

Over and above that, and even more important, is the meditation or spiritual work in which each student engages to the end, that citizens are not swayed by the carnal mind and the highly charged emotional promotional activities characteristic of a typical presidential campaign. Each student should realize that the universal human mind, with its lust for power, greed, and self-seeking, is not power in the realized presence of God; that this election, as an activity for the preservation of freedom, is taking place within the one Consciousness, which is Intelligence and Love, and that only *I* votes. That *I* is the divine Consciousness, individualized. It is guided by a wisdom beyond human understanding and is, therefore, unerring in Its judgment.

The Foundation of Freedom

No one can guarantee you, as American citizens, freedom, except yourselves. And if you study the issues of your political life to such an extent and with such a clarity of thought that you can go to the polls and vote intelligently, that freedom will continue. And if not, be assured of this: If you allow the mesmerism of the press, of newspapers, of fanaticism, or whatnot in the political field to sway your minds, it won't be too long until the freedoms, which have been guaranteed you, will be found missing.

Our political freedom is one that was dearly bought in this country, and it has taken all of the efforts of many men and many women to hold on to it. Many times it's been endangered, never more than in recent years. And the struggle has been hard to hold it. Only time will tell whether or not freedom is to be a permanent thing in the United States of America. Benjamin Franklin did say, when he turned over this document of freedom to the United States, "You have been given your freedom, but I wonder, will you be able to hold it?"[3] And that question can well be asked today. Will America be able to hold its freedom?

Now, this is much more true when you come to the spiritual universe because to find your spiritual freedom and to hold it is even more difficult than securing and holding on to political and economic freedom. The reason is this: You can have committees, and you can have Congresses, and you can have Supreme Courts to watch over your political freedom. You can have Reserve Banks, and you can have great financiers to watch over your economic freedom, but you can't have a board of directors, you can't even have a minister or a priest or a teacher to watch over your spiritual freedom. No one can achieve that for you but yourself. No one can hold it for you but yourself.

Place the freedom of the world in the hands of the Infinite. Take it out of the hands of man and realize that this world is not at the mercy of sin or stupidity. If we return the authority to the divine Consciousness, then this freedom, this "idea whose time has come,"[4] will express itself.

The life we live as Infinite Way students is really not a religious life as religion is usually thought of. It is a contemplative life, the life in which we ponder, meditate, and cogitate upon Reality. It is a life in which we commune with our inner or spiritual Self. It is a life which, by means of receptivity, makes us responsive to impartations from the Infinite to the individual. It is a life in which we look to the divine Source for our good, a life in which we are not enslaved by words. Too often, a word gets a grip on us, and then we are the victims of that word, such words as "he," "she," or "it." In fact, all evil is bound up in these words. But what we must do is to look beyond every "he," "she," and "it" in the world and realize:

God is the source of my good. God is the source of my supply. God is the cement of my relationships.

In such moments we will be looking over the heads of those who are venal in their conduct, those who are merely selfish, and those who are neither venal nor selfish but who are ignorant, and thanking God that freedom is not at the mercy of any of these, that freedom is the gift of God, and it is God who establishes freedom on earth as it is in heaven. Then, instead of becoming angry at some "he," "she," or "it," any sense of anger is directed at ourselves for being enslaved by the "he," "she," or "it."

This nation was not founded on men, but by men. It was founded on principles of freedom, equality, justice, and only the activity of the Christ has enabled this nation to go through these nearly two centuries, standing firmly for these principles. Only the activity of the Christ will enable those now in office, and those to come, to be inspired, that these principles may endure. In government, as in religion, the men, the leaders will come, and they will go, but when nations or religions are founded on principles, the nations and the religions will continue forever.

Our Birthright of Freedom

Are we not heirs of God? Do we not have jurisdiction over our lives by the grace of God? Are we not servants of God? And if we are, how could we ever become servants of man, or slaves of man, or slaves of a system?

These things can only creep up on us by our consent. And the only way we give our consent is by ignoring our relationship with God. Our freedom must be spiritually attained, spiritually realized, spiritually maintained, and then "nothing can enter that defileth or maketh a lie."[5] Nothing can enter from without. No powers external to us can operate in our consciousness or upon our lives except by our ignorance of spiritual truth, spiritual identity, and the fact that freedom isn't a physical thing; it's a spiritual entity.

Now be assured of this: If you hold freedom to be something of a physical nature that can be given to you or taken from you, so will it be unto you in accordance with your faith. But in that moment when you realize only by the grace of God do we have freedom, only by the grace of God do we have God's government and that this is not at the mercy of "man whose breath is in his nostrils,"[6] that this cannot be given to us by princes nor taken from us by kings or potentates—only by the realization of the spiritual nature of freedom can we attain it and maintain it.

Freedom is not a condition of mind or body. Freedom is a condition of the Soul. If we do not find our freedom in Soul, we will find only limitation and bondage in our experience. Freedom cannot be given to a nation or a race of people. Freedom must first be realized in individual being, and then some measure of that freedom can be shared with those who are in need of it.

Nothing external to us can limit or hinder us because our freedom must first take place in our consciousness, and this, no one can prevent because fortunately no one can read our thoughts, look into our consciousness, or know what is going on in our soul. So it is that wherever we are—at home, on the street, or in business—we can make a transition from the slavery of the senses to the freedom of the Soul. It all takes place within our consciousness.

The message of The Infinite Way revealed to me at the beginning that God does not set us free. It is the consciousness of God in us that makes us free. Where the consciousness of the presence of God is not, there is bondage; there is sin, false appetite, disease, lack, limitation, and man's inhumanity to man. But where the consciousness of God is present—not where God is present—God is omnipresence. Where the consciousness of God is present, there is liberty, freedom, wholeness, completeness.

So carry the consciousness of God with you. Carry it up to heaven if you mount there, because you will not find God in heaven unless you carry Him there. Carry the consciousness of God to hell if your pathway leads you there. Carry the consciousness of the presence of God into disease, into death, into hospitals, into mental institutions. Carry the consciousness of the presence of God into your buses.

Above all, carry it into your polling places when you go to vote, or you may not find the right man elected because "man whose breath is in his nostrils" has a very great habit of selecting the wrong man. But the presence of God makes no mistake.

The Choice: Dominion or Domination

> For unto us a child is born, unto us a son is given: and the government shall be upon his shoulder: and his name shall be called Wonderful, Counsellor, The mighty God, The everlasting Father, The Prince of Peace.
>
> Isaiah 9:6

This moment we must choose whether we will serve God or man. Are we to be God-governed or man-governed this year? If we are true to God, we need have no fear that we will be untrue to man, to our government, or to any government that stands for individual freedom, liberty, justice, and for the integrity of individual being. Therefore, we take our stand for government under God.

But what does government under God mean? First of all, it means that we must acknowledge that "God has given to us his only begotten Son,"[7] and the function of this Presence that has been planted in the midst of us is to "go before us to make the crooked places straight."[8] It is to go before us "to prepare mansions"[9] for us.

> *God-life and my life are one, inseparable, indivisible, and incorporeal, not at the mercy of "man, whose breath is in his nostrils," not at the mercy of "princes,"[10] but a divine life lived under God. "I and my Father are one,"[11] incorporeal and invisible. I "live, and move, and have my being"[12] in God. I live and have my being in Spirit, in the Soul of God, in the Spirit of God. I am "hid with Christ in God."[13] This is my fortress; this is my dwelling place—to live, move, and have my being in Spirit, under spiritual government.*

By not consciously taking hold of our own lives and opening ourselves to God-government, we leave ourselves to the government of "this world." That means we accept ourselves as a statistic. We are a hundred people, and out of these hundred people, so many must die each day, and so many must become ill, so many must have an accident. And the question mark is, which one of us will this happen to, which one of us will that happen to, and on what day?

The inevitability of sin, disease, death, lack, and limitation is always present for the simple reason that by not consciously accepting the government of God, we unconsciously or subconsciously accept anything that is blowing around in the air. And therefore, if a newspaper headline tells of a coming epidemic, then so many immediately prepare, unconsciously, for it. If the newspapers or radio are full of fear about coming world conditions, that fear operates in consciousness to set up ills of one nature or another. So it is that actually the human race—each individual—is an antenna receiving whatever is being broadcast of the world's fears, of the world's sins, of the world's false appetites and diseases. And men and women in the human experience have no defense against the acceptance of the suggestions of the world.

The three dimensional man, the man of earth, lives in a world circumscribed by his own limited concept of himself and his world, believing that that is all the world there is and that in order to survive, it is necessary to lie, cheat, and to use all the tricks of the trade even up to and including warfare. To him, might is a right and normal way, and anything else is a sign of weakness.

This is the life lived by the man who is ignorant of the truth that there is another realm of consciousness which he could enter and there, find a more glorious life, one not lived by might or by power, a world in which he could live at peace with his neighbors, with his competitors, and with all other races and religions on the face of the earth.

As a human being, as the man of earth, "the natural man, who is not under the law of God,"[14] you have no dominion in this world whatsoever. You are acted upon by weather, by climate, by food, if you want to accept it, even by the stars above you. You are acted upon, and this is not the natural way of living, the spiritual way. The spiritual way of life gives you dominion. God gave you dominion over this entire earth and everything beneath and everything above. Now, to live under grace, you must make a conscious effort, through knowing the truth, to bring yourself back to the position where you have dominion.

Right now, I acknowledge that "this is the day the Lord hath made,"[15] and I give this day to God, and I surrender myself to God. I give over the government of my body, of my business, of my home, of my art, or my profession to God. I recognize that there is an invisible Something in this world, that men call "God," and that if I am imbued with It, I will be a better businessman, or better artist, or better professional person. My affairs will prosper if I do not try to do it alone. "Except the Lord build the house, they labour in vain that build it."[16] Except the Lord build the house.

And so whatever "house" I have to build today, if now I open my consciousness to God's presence, to God's grace, to God's health, it is inevitable that I will build a better day, do a better business, be more successful in my music, or painting, or whatever my activity may be.

In our work, we start it this way. Before we start our day's work, before we can become a victim of the world, we start our earliest morning period by assuming our God-given dominion, realizing that "this is the day the Lord hath made." This is the day that God will govern this earth. God will govern mankind. God will govern all that pertains to man. God's government will be supreme. God's government alone will rule my day, my home, my business, my health, and all who will open themselves to God's government and God's dominion. But this must be an act of your consciousness. You must negate the world's dominion over you and its laws, and you must, by an act of consciousness, bring the law of God into your experience.

Now, with this alone, we have brought the kingdom of God to earth whereas without it, we have left the kingdom of God anywhere else except in our own experience.

The Inner Kingdom and Inner Power

Many of the problems the world faces are humanly insoluble, problems of such magnitude that they are beyond the mind or brain, even of those who seek the highest offices in the nations of the world. This is a time that shakes man's faith. This is a time when people begin to think and fear and doubt. Yet this is our great opportunity. Why? Do we have a solution to these problems? Not any human solution.

Heaven forbid that anybody in this age should any longer believe that any government of man is going to establish peace on earth or peace among men or the stability in human relationships necessary to harmonious living.

The Master did not have a human solution to offer in his day. And yet he did have a solution for every problem of human experience. He taught recourse to an inner kingdom, an inner power that makes men free.

"The kingdom of God is within you."[17] That is our Master's message. "The kingdom of God is within you," and this kingdom is not a temporal kingdom; it is a spiritual kingdom. But, when the spiritual kingdom is set up in our consciousness, it changes the whole nature of the outer universe and brings in its turn all of those freedoms for which we are struggling.

Regardless of where you live, or under what form of government, or under what form of religious activity, you must set up within yourself the kingdom that is to free you from human domination, from the domination of "man whose breath is in his nostrils." You must set up that kingdom within yourself, and it must be a spiritual kingdom.

You are no more outside of God's government than the stars, the sun, the moon, the tides, the fish swimming in the sea, or the birds flying in the air. Relax into the awareness that there is a creative, maintaining, and sustaining Principle of life, and It is holding this world in Its grasp. Then you will be able to smile at the intrigues of men who believe they have the power to set aside the laws of God, to destroy the life of God or the freedom and harmony of God, or to interfere with the operation of God.

There is the thought: Can you conceive of anything that can interfere with the operation of God? Then, when you wonder at the evils you have witnessed on earth, you will know it has been our ignorance of this truth that has brought these catastrophes upon us. We have not understood that God is not influenced by man, but rather that God governs man and all creation. God alone governs, and God does not share His government with "man whose breath is in his nostrils, for he isn't even to be accounted of."

There isn't a single law of matter or mind that can stand up as law in the experience of one who can begin to understand the universal nature of God governing Its universe and not permitting any interference with Its government. Think of trying to interfere with God's government of this universe, and we know it cannot be done. Therefore, when we suffer, we are suffering only from these mental images that have been thrown at us, which we, in our ignorance, have accepted.

Obedient Awareness

God is the "author and finisher"[18] of our work, of our world. And if we look to God, the one Mind, the infinite Intelligence, and the divine Love of this universe, we will find that regardless of what any individual or group of individuals may appear to be doing in any given moment, in the final analysis, the decision rests with the great author, God, the one Mind, and the one Soul of the entire universe.

Since God is the Mind of individual man, it follows that man can only carry out the lines given to him by the great author. Since the nature of that Mind is love, truth, principle, it necessarily follows that only such qualities and only such activities can become a part of our universe.

Right here let me say that it is true that there are many people in the world who do not know that they receive their lines directly from the author and that they are but the vehicles for the carrying out of the divine plan, and these people have set up the word "I," or "me," or "mine" within themselves, and they live out from the basis of "I," "me," or "mine," and thereby bring themselves ultimately to disaster since no one in and of himself can write his part.

It takes the mind of the great author, the great architect of the universe, to plan and to direct, and as we become obedient to that direction, we find our lives God-governed, harmoniously maintained and sustained.

In my personal experience, I have witnessed the larger proof of this work in some, what we call "capital and labor experiences," corporation and union activities. I have seen this, where one side—in some cases, it was the capital side, and in other cases, it was the labor side—was willing to call in the power of spiritual prayer and abide by it, and harmony resulted without the use of force and with a joyous result for everyone concerned.

I have also witnessed it in some of the affairs concerning our government in the States where, on certain occasions when serious evils looked ready to befall, the power of this conscious realization of God resulted in the overcoming of that experience. I can tell you one such experience very quickly.

The Congress of the United States had been made a rubber stamp and was not functioning as a Congress. It had surrendered its powers to the president, and it accepted his bills and rubber-stamped them into being, and that was that! The only thing that stood between free government and dictatorship was the Supreme Court of the United States. With that out of the way, we would have had a totalitarian form of government. The president would have governed without a Congress and without a Supreme Court to stop him.

Now, he'd already eliminated Congress; he still had the Supreme Court in his way, and he evolved a perfect scheme of doing away with it. Instead of nine men on the board whom he couldn't influence or buy or throw out, he decided to have a bill passed in Congress, increasing the Supreme Court to a membership of fifteen, which meant that he would appoint six stooges on it. And with those, he would control the Supreme Court and put it out of existence, and we would have had a totalitarian form of government.

One night while that bill was due for consideration, sitting in my home in meditation—not about it, I had no thought of it, my mind was on realizing God—the Voice said to me, "Do not go to bed tonight; sit up and pray about that Supreme Court bill!" I said, "Yes, Father." And I sat there merely attaining a conscious union with God. I had no words to use; I didn't outline what was to happen, whether the bill should succeed or fail. It had nothing to do with that. I had only one function to perform that night, and that was to attain a conscious union with God, the experience of knowing that God was on the field, and all is well. At four o'clock in the morning, that happened. At four o'clock in the morning, all of a sudden, a great peace descended upon me, and I knew that all was well, and I retired.

Well, the next day, the senator who was in charge of presenting that bill, putting it through Congress, went to the President of the United States and said, "Mr. President, I'm sorry. I can't betray my country. I won't put that bill through." Sometime later, we discovered, a prominent editor, newspaper editor of a chain of papers, said that he awakened out of sleep at four o'clock in the morning and that a voice said to him, "Get busy; that Supreme Court bill means slavery!" He jumped out of bed, put on the teletype, "Headlines: Stop the Supreme Court Bill." And he did. Every other newspaper had to follow suit when he did. That Supreme Court bill never did go through.

> Know ye not, that to whom ye yield yourselves servants to obey, his servants ye are to whom ye obey …
>
> Romans 6:16

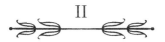

II

THE GENESIS OF IDENTITY

THERE ARE TWO levels of consciousness. There is the spiritual, incorporeal level, as described in the first chapter of Genesis. On this level, man created in the image and likeness of God shows forth neither sin, disease, death, lack, limitation, nor any of man's inhumanity to man. Those born into the consciousness of the first chapter of Genesis have neither father nor mother. They are the Melchizedek-consciousness: they are not physical offspring, and they have no human parentage. They are incorporeal. But those born of human parents are born into the level of the second-chapter-of-Genesis creation, the world of mind, the mortal consciousness of good and evil, which constitutes humanhood. It is this humanhood that makes us think that by destroying our enemy or competitor, we can live and prosper, or that by taking away somebody's freedom, we can become greater. A leaven is necessary to break through the crust of self-preservation. This leaven is the Spirit of God in man, which, when It is raised up, lifts man to Its level, and then, instead of "man whose breath is in his nostrils,"[1] we now have the Son of God, that "man who has his being in Christ."[2] The Master acknowledged that there are two men: the man of earth—the creature, the mortal, the viper—and the divine Presence within individual consciousness, which,

15

when recognized and released, changes man from the man of earth to the Son of God.

We speak of God as the creative principle of this entire universe, including man. But actually, that brings up a picture in your mind of a God that created something at some time, and as long as you hold to that belief, you cannot rightly understand the nature of God, for God has never created any thing at any time. Any such belief puts God in time and space, and with a beginning, and that takes away God's eternality and immortality. I ask you rather, see God as an Infinite Invisible, appearing *as* this universe, rather than as starting it, creating it, or making it at a time.

Let us use the illustration now of the fruit tree. As you watch the fruit appear on your tree, you could say, "Ah, there is God in the act of creation." But that wouldn't literally be true because that creation began before the fruit was visible. There was fruit there when it was still in the invisible—when it was, let us say, sap in the tree. But even that wouldn't be right to say that creation began with the sap, because before there was sap, there were elements in the ground which some action of life drew into the roots of the tree that went to form the sap that went up into the tree and formed the bud and fruit. But it wouldn't be right to say that creation began with the drawing of the substances in, because the substances were in the ground before the drawing began. And so if you keep going back and back and back again, you'll find that you cannot locate in time or space when that fruit began to be created that was going to appear on your tree. And, if you go back far enough, you'd find that when it really began was when God began.

In other words, God did not create in the sense that man can create this object because when you have this object, you have man, the inventor or manufacturer, and an object. But when you have this universe, you haven't got God and a universe. There's no God, standing separate and apart from the universe, looking off into a universe which He created. God is the substance and law of this created universe. Therefore, it is more accurate to say, "God appears as this universe. God unfolds Himself as this universe."

When you begin to see this, you'll know that God isn't a power here, creating a universe here, nor is God a power here, patching up a universe. There's no such thing. God is the very life, law, and substance that appears on your tree as fruit. God is the very life, law, substance, and activity that appears in your hand as your baby. God is the very law and life and activity and substance that appears to us as ourselves, each other, and this universe. And the creating never began. It is a continuous unfoldment of God revealing Himself throughout all time.

When you see that, you do not think of God as a power to which you can turn now, and ask God, "Heal this body," or "Put fruit on my tree," or "Bring me supply." You can't do that if you understand the nature of God. All you can do is realize omnipresence. The very moment you say, "God is," you have prayed the prayer of all the ages that results in a harmonious demonstration. God is. What is God? God is Life. Whose life? Well, surely not my life and not your life. If my life, then it must be your life. If my life, then it must be the life of the tree since God is one. "Hear, O Israel: the Lord our God, the Lord He is one."[3] And the Master said, "Acknowledge only one God."[4] Yes, but God is Life. Well then, acknowledge only one life. But God is Love. Then acknowledge only one love. But God is Law. Then acknowledge only one law.

When you acknowledge God as one law, you can then say, "Well, then material law, physical law—why they must be instruments of that one." They can't be destructive to that one. They must be offshoots of that one, just as if you want to call your body a physical body, you may. Actually, it's a spiritual body, because it's formed of the substance of God since God could not be infinite and then have a God and your body, separate and apart from God. Your body would have to be included in the substance of which God is formed. God made all that was made, and anything that God did not make was not made.

Never forget that this life of yours is God, and if it appears to you to be young or old, sick or well, evil or good, that is just God appearing to you, but incorrectly interpreted by you. You are the one who must reinterpret the scene. There is no use going about saying, "Oh, I know there is no old age, sickness, or evil in heaven, but what about earth?" Heaven and earth are not two different places. Heaven and earth are one and the same: earth is our mortal concept of heaven, and heaven is our real awareness of the earth. In other words, heaven is the earth correctly understood.

Now follow this carefully. Here are two important points: right identification which means God appearing as individual life, the One appearing as many, or God, Life, appearing as individual being; and reinterpretation, which means looking at sick, sinning, dying humanity, and translating that appearance through the realization that inasmuch as God is all, this is part of the allness of God which is being mis-seen, coming as a false suggestion, which must be reinterpreted.

These two important points must be carried with you from morning to night and night to morning: right identification and reinterpretation. Reinterpret everything you see, hear, taste, touch, and smell. Reinterpret it! Translate it into its original state, which is Godhood; practice right identification.

Heir of God

The understanding of our spiritual identity will solve all of the problems of the world because, with right identification, the principles of spiritual living will be revealed. These principles cannot be revealed, however, until we discover right identity and learn to commune with the Soul—your Soul and my Soul. It is within the Soul that the mysteries of life are hidden, and it is through the Soul that they are revealed.

The moment we become reconciled to and at-one with our Source, then, immediately, we are "heirs, joint-heirs" to all the heavenly riches. In my reconciliation, it is necessary to know not only that I am the heir of God, but I must also know that I am joint-heir with you, so that I include you in that divine sonship. In my reconciliation with God and with you, I am fulfilled. In that state of reconciliation, we pass from the man of earth to "that man who has his being in Christ."

Right identity, right identification, is the most important step in one's spiritual development. As long as you believe yourself to be man, you will be on the receiving end of both good and evil, a little and a lot, life and death. And the very moment you realize I am not man, I am Soul, I am Spirit, I

am Consciousness, I am *I*, then, in that moment, you have
your God-given dominion over the flesh, over everything
on earth and beneath the earth and in the air above and in
the skies above.

Remember, the promise is that you are to bear fruit richly
because of your identification with God, your Father within
you. Once this has been established in you, you now have
to begin secretly, silently, and very sacredly to look around
at the members of your household and at your friends and
begin to change your concepts of them so that you realize
that all this that you have been declaring of yourself is
likewise true of them. They, too, are one with this divine
Selfhood. The fact that at the moment they do not know
it is not your concern. You are not dealing with their
demonstration but with your own, and you will not have
any kind of demonstration unless you begin to perceive that
this truth that you have declared and realized about yourself
must be a universal truth.

Regardless of any person's lack of demonstration,
regardless of his unwillingness even to want to learn about
his true identity, you are secretly and silently knowing
the truth. You know the true identity of your employers,
employees, your customers or clients, and the officials of the
government. It makes no difference what these persons may
seem to be or may seem to be doing. You realize their oneness
with their Source. It is not for the purpose of giving them a
treatment, but to save yourself from being a malpractitioner,
because unless you are seeing people as they really are, you
are malpracticing them, and your malpractice eventually
comes home to roost. Your malpractice of other persons
never harms them, and their malpractice of you never harms
you. Any malpractice acts as a boomerang: it goes out from

us and eventually hits nothing because it is aimed only at our concept of a person—not at the person—and, therefore, it turns around and returns and cuts our heads off. It never strikes those at whom it is aimed. It always turns around and reacts upon the sender.

Mistaken Identity

We all want to be understood and to be understanding. Most of us wish that those we meet could see into the center of our being, could see what we have been from the beginning, but which no one has yet recognized—not mother, not father, not teacher. No one has ever seen what we really are, and it is because of this nonrecognition that we have worn a mask to hide ourselves from the world. If only the mask that is hiding you from me and me from you could drop from our faces, we would be like children, back in the Garden of Eden. Everyone longs to be understood, but most persons think that that means being known as they are humanly. That is not what it means at all. Those who believe that do so because they do not yet know that the Christ is their true identity, and this is really what they would like to show forth.

The Master, Christ Jesus, too, longed to have his true identity recognized and understood. How obvious is his longing as he asks, "Whom do men say that I the son of man am? Who say ye that I am?"[5] He longed to be known as the Christ, but he could not walk out and say, "I am the Christ." Let us not hesitate, however, to say silently and secretly to everyone we meet, "Thou art the Christ, the holy one of Israel.[6] I know thee who thou art."[7]

How do we know it? Flesh and blood have not taught us this, nor has the human mind revealed it. Only spiritual discernment reveals to us that God lives on earth as individual you and me. God has incarnated Himself as individual being. God, the Father, appears on earth as God, the Son. As we begin the practice of beholding the Christ in everyone we meet—in our household, our neighborhood, the market, the post office, the department store—the world will begin to present a different picture to us. People will act in a different way. The world will respond differently to us because the world will bring back to us what we have given to it.

We have identified ourselves with the body instead of knowing that we are not the body. We are really the soul of the body, the life of the body, the mind of the body, the spirit of the body, the consciousness of the body. But we are not the body; we are as incorporeal as God, for God is Spirit, and His son must be spiritual. Just think what a shock some of our students will have when they realize that. Then you'll know what a shock the rest of the world will have when it wakes up to the fact that we are really incorporeal being; that we have all of the nature, quality, and character of God; that we are the offspring of God; that God has embodied within us all of Himself: "Son, all that I have is thine[8]; the very place whereon thou standest is holy ground,"[9] for God is there. God is here as my being, as your being, and God is Spirit: your being, my being. It is Spirit.

Let me remind you that we do not know the truth about man in our work. We do not know the truth about you. We do not know the truth about a human being. Our prayer and treatment work is knowing the truth about Truth, knowing the truth about God.

What differentiates the life of the person who experiences good and evil, health and sickness, abundance and lack, purity and sin, happiness and unhappiness, from the life of the person of spiritual attainment, whose life is, on the whole, a continuity of harmony, is the matter of right identification. Right identification is a recognition of the truth that *I* is God and the ability not to think out from the standpoint of being man, limited and subject to human laws.

Ignorance of our true identity is the only cause of error in our experience. In proportion as we regain the Father's house—that's the experience of the prodigal—as we determine to return to the Father's house, the Father-consciousness, and realize, "Why God, the Father, is my consciousness; God, the Father, is the author of my life, the architect of my life; therefore, my life must show forth the perfection of its creator," then do we begin to restore harmony through spiritual realization.

The search for truth has always and ever been a search for a way to return to God-consciousness.

When Are We
Under God's Government?

Remember that "the man of flesh cannot please God"[10] and cannot be under God's government. Who is the man of flesh? The man who lives by the human code of Moses: "An eye for an eye and a tooth for a tooth,"[11] or seeking to live by the sword, or seeking to invoke human weapons instead of spiritual armor, which is the word of God.

"But ye are children of God."[12] When? When you "bless your enemies, love your enemies, bless them that curse you, do good to them that hate you, pray for them which despitefully use you and persecute you. Then ye are the children of your Father, which is in heaven."[13] That's all there is to this. It's a matter of law or grace. "Choose ye this day whom you will serve"[14]: to live under the law, or to live under grace.

Watch the Sermon on the Mount. It is a guide to two ways of living. You can choose the one you like best: the law or grace. If you choose the law, you will temporarily have a little easier time of it because you will be conforming to common usage; you'll be going right along with the crowd, right in the swim.

On the other hand, if you attempt to live by grace, you will find yourself out of step with this world. You will find yourself peculiar; you'll find yourself sometimes taking losses that you're not entitled to; you'll find yourself sometimes suffering from injustices that you don't deserve. It doesn't deny that for a minute here. In fact, it encourages you to do those very things, because, in the end, you'll find you're under God's grace, God's government, God's protection. God's will is being done in you, not the will of man. That's an entirely different life.

Right here and now, I accept the grace of God. I accept the grace of God as the allness and onlyness and perfection of my being, of my body, of my business. I accept God's grace as companionship, as home, as opportunity, as success. I accept, consciously, the grace of God as a law unto my being—as the only law, the only law operating in my mind, in my consciousness, in my heart, in my life, in my soul, in my being, in my body, in all that concerns me. I consciously accept God as the one influence in my life. I accept the activity of the Christ, the spirit of Soul. I accept the love of God as the only love in my experience. I consciously reject any love which is not of God. I consciously reject every love which is not of God, every law which is not of God, every belief which is not of God, anything and everything of a material and a mental nature which is not of God. And in doing this, I open myself to receive divine grace in consciousness, to accept the government of God in place of the government of matter and material beliefs and mental beliefs, mortal beliefs and theories, and superstitions.

Why should I be under the subject of where the stars are in the sky? Why should I be under the superstitions of a church? Why should I be under the superstitions of astrology or theology? Why should I even be under the superstitions of natural law? Why not, in my inner consciousness, realize,

God's government is supreme, and it operates through grace. And I, here and now, accept the grace of God.

Now having done this once, thoroughly and completely, we have at least made room within ourselves to remind ourselves every time that there is the appearance of something contrary to that. We again remind ourselves that it's the grace of God that governs me, not material law, not mental law, and we remind ourselves that spiritual power emanates from within my being and flows out from me to my affairs.

Therefore, nothing in the outer realm can act upon me, whether it's the stars in the sky or the bombs in the sky. "Nothing from without can enter that defileth or maketh a lie,"[15] but all good flows out from me, through me, to me and all who are within range of my consciousness.

That is an activity of truth in consciousness that we must practice, and we must practice it continuously until one beautiful day comes along when all of a sudden, something happens within, and when it does, you say, "Oh, just think! That was all true. Heretofore I've declared it, but now I know it." There's a difference between declaring it and knowing it. Once it is known, you no more have to declare it than you would walk around declaring your name or declaring that 2 x 2 is 4, or declaring that your money is in your right-hand pocket. You don't have to declare anything once you know it. I mean by that, know it with this inner conviction that is called "spiritual discernment," and that comes in that second of transition when the Christ takes over, announces itself, reveals itself as being on the field and in possession of all of your being and body and business.

You will be surprised at the change that takes place in your life once you have, shall we say, reasoned this through, or worked and practiced with it until you have come to an actual conviction that God is Spirit, that God is invisible, and that the law of God must be a spiritual law, and that this must be the all-power. You see, from the moment that you can even intellectually agree that this must be truth, from that moment on, changes begin to appear, but much more so when, through holding to this truth, maintaining this truth in your consciousness, abiding in it and letting it abide in you, you eventually come to that point of conviction, that point in which you say, "Ah, before I was blind, but now I see. Before, I may have intellectually agreed, but now I spiritually know and discern: God is Spirit." Therefore, the government of this universe, the government of your individual life, the government of your collective life must be spiritual.

You can watch this work out even in your politics, where, if you will not put your faith in the candidates whom you vote for, and if you will not put your faith in the parties they represent, even while fulfilling your human obligation of choosing the candidate you believe to be best fitted, and casting your vote according to your highest sense of right—even while doing this—if you will realize that the real government that is to come through these men is spiritual; the real government is upon His shoulder, the Christ. The real dominion of this world is the dominion of God, not the domination of men, but the dominion of God.

Actually, it would make no difference if we elected the wrong candidates—if there is such a thing as right ones or wrong ones—if, in doing so, we at the same time realized, "I'm not putting my hope, faith, or confidence in you but in the divine government which will operate in you and through you."

In other words, I accept God as the only power; I accept God as the only lawgiver, the only government, and that's spiritual. Then I can trust God to exercise His judgment through the mind or consciousness of individual man. And that destroys the power of the human mind and human thought. It deprives an individual of the power to misapply his office.

It is when we look to "man whose breath is in his nostrils" and believe, "You are my salvation. I'm looking to you to run this country or this state or this city," or, "I am expecting the principles of your party to save us"—only then are you subject to the domination of man. But if you can look behind this scene and acknowledge God, but acknowledge God as omnipotent, acknowledge God as law and lawgiver, acknowledge God as Spirit and God's law as spiritual, and

the government on His shoulder, you will have men first
governed by God, and then our government governed by
men who are governed by God.

See Him as He Is

The whole of the spiritual path is an internal struggle
that takes place within our consciousness. It isn't what's
wrong with the world. There's nothing wrong with the
world. What is wrong with my concept of the world?
How am I beholding the world? Am I seeing Jesus as a
resurrected Hebrew prophet, or am I seeing Jesus as Peter
saw him, as the Christ? Am I seeing man as a mortal, or am
I recognizing Christ incarnate? Do you see the difference?
And, it's as simple as this, and it's as difficult as this. The
simplicity is that there are only two important parts: the
nature of God and His creation, the nature of error and its
creation, and that's all. We build our entire life on those two
points.

When you are thinking of a member of your family or
some of the politicians—and I use that word in its worst
sense—or when you think of the so-called dictators of the
world, remember that the *I* in the midst of them is knocking
at the door of your consciousness for entrance. Do not open
your consciousness to their humanhood because you are
opening your consciousness to an illusory picture. Rather
open your consciousness to the *I* of every individual.

The sad part is that most persons keep right on seeing
those around them as they appear to be and pin the very
errors on them that they dislike; whereas if only they could
see the word "*I*" over the heads of each one of them and
realize that the *I* of them is knocking at the door of their

consciousness for recognition, they would be lifting them out of these errors.

If we insist on seeing each other as the man of earth, as mortal man—some good, some bad, some well, some sick—then it is the world we are creating for ourselves. But if we have been granted any degree of spiritual discernment so that we can behold the *I* of every individual and receive It into our consciousness, acknowledge It, welcome It, and bless It, then we transform our world.

You can face any situation that arises in your life— anything from a family situation, to a national or an international situation—if you can learn to sit quietly with it, and lift up the *I*. Lift up the *I* and realize, that as long as you are abiding in that *I*, as long as you are abiding in that Presence, "no evil can come nigh this world." In My presence is fulfillment. In My presence, in the presence of God, is fullness of life. And as long as you have the presence of *I* lifted up in you, it isn't only that evil can't come nigh thy dwelling place, it can't come nigh thy entire world.

It wasn't for pleasure or pastime that Scripture reveals that "one with God is a majority,"[16] or that even "two or more gathered together in my name,"[17] or that "ten righteous men can save a city."[18] We don't have to wait for three billion people to learn this truth to save the world. A little handful of us can uphold this *I*, can live with this *I* up here, face the world with It always, and watch the evils of this world dissolve in the consciousness of personal enemies, national enemies, international enemies. But somebody must hold up the banner of *I*. Somebody must admit the *I* that is knocking at the door of this whole world, seeking entrance.

Now, let us go beyond this room; let us go beyond each of us individually, and let us remember that this *I*, of which I have been talking, is God. The *I* is knocking at the door of this entire world at this minute and begging to be admitted, and all we have to do, a little of us, a group of us—is to open this world to the presence of *I*. Open the door and say, "Father come in, for in Thy presence, there is no warfare; in Thy presence is peace; in Thy presence is fulfillment."

And, open the door of your consciousness, open the door of this universe, and admit God. For this world is suffering from only one thing: the absence of God. It either doesn't believe that the Messiah has yet come, or it believes that we are waiting for the Messiah to come. And all the while, It is saying to us, "*I* am standing at the door and begging, begging to be admitted." And all we have to do is open our consciousness and say, "Father, enter. Enter this world. Enter human consciousness."

Let us acknowledge that there is an *I* knocking at the door of this world. Let us open the door and admit God, and you will soon see how rapidly the sins, the diseases, the lacks, and the limitations of this world will disappear because in My presence is fulfillment. "My peace I give unto you."[19] How can *I* give it to you if you don't admit Me into your consciousness? How can *I* give it to you?

Open the door of your consciousness; open the door of this world. Let the Father in, and watch the silent, sacred, secret influence as It permeates all human consciousness and eventually reveals peace. Peace won't come through man; peace won't come through treaties; peace won't come through armament; peace won't come through disarmament. Peace will only come through opening the door of consciousness and letting Me, the Father, in.

"I Must Meet the Rent"

Now, you remember how much of the Master's ministry was involved in that statement that "the government shall be on his shoulder."[20] When the kingdom of God shall come on earth, "the government shall be on his shoulder."

Will the government of God ever come on earth as a collective thing? Not very likely, as long as there's a personal sense of I. But the government of God does come on earth every moment of every day to somebody. Somewhere in this world, every moment of every day, somebody is saying, "Why the government is on Its shoulder. Let It run Its universe. Let Him run His universe." And that moment, they have brought the kingdom of God to earth in their individual experience. They can't bring it in yours or mine because giving up the personal sense of I is an individual thing that concerns you or me, and we can't do it for each other.

Why, if I had such power, I'd just wave a wand and say, "Now, all my students, you have no more 'I' to contend with, and that means you have no more problems." You know I'd love to do that, but I can't. There is no such power. Jesus couldn't. He said, "If I go not away, this realization, this Comforter, cannot come to you,"[21] because I can't do this for you. I cannot make you give up the word "I."

I cannot make you give up your concern for the word "I," even though I say to you, "You are a child of God; if a child, then an heir; if an heir, joint-heir with Christ in God,"[22] and that makes you heir to all the riches in heaven and on earth. Why should you take thought now for next month's supply?

And I say that to you, but that's all that I can do about it. I cannot make you stop saying, "Oh, but I must meet the rent." That is what happens in practitioners' offices all the time. They will sit and sit and sit and voice truth and voice truth, and after an hour, the patient will say, "Oh yes, but I have such pain. Oh, yes, but I must meet the rent. Oh, yes, but I don't know what to do." Well, there isn't anything anyone can do because the entire problem is involved in that word "I," and it's involved in giving up the use of the word "I" in that sense.

The word "*I*" means God. That should be clear in everyone's mind, in every student's mind. The word "*I*" means God. It never means Joel. It always means God. True, it means God appearing as Joel. Therefore, Joel is always God-governed, God-maintained, God-sustained, because it is really God maintaining Its own identity as Joel, just like nature maintains its own identity as a rose, as an orchid, as a tulip, as a violet, as a lily, but it's always nature maintaining its own identity *as*. Or, mathematics maintains its identity as one, two, three, four, five, but it is mathematics maintaining the quality and quantity of each figure. So with music—it is the principle of music that always maintains and sustains the separate identity called "do, re, me," and so forth.

It is God that maintains God's own identity as me and as you. The government is on God's shoulder to maintain Itself and to sustain Itself.

Expansion of Identity as a Spiritual Citizen

In the materialistic way of life, it is a natural thing, humanly, for us to be proud of being American, Canadian, English, German, or whatever our nationality may be. But what happens to that swashbuckling materialism when we discover our Self, when we discover that we all are brothers and sisters, regardless of the flag that flies over us, the color of our skin, or the church to which we belong, and realize,

Never am I limited to a country, to a nation, or a state. I am limited only to the kingdom of God, and there I am of the household of God, heir of God, and joint-heir with every spiritual being in this great wide world of ours, of one great family, one great spiritual brotherhood.

To rise above the limitations of personal sense does not make us any less good citizens; in fact, it makes us better citizens, but better citizens because we respect the citizenship of other persons. Real citizenship is to live in fellowship, but this cannot be experienced until the nature of our true identity is understood, and then, whether we are Jew or Greek, bond or free, we are all of one spiritual household.

Ultimately, we shall all discover that our true identity is Christ, and although we may have been brought up as Jones, Brown, or Smith, our real name, our identity, and our potentiality, is Christ, the spiritual offspring of God. In the moment that this truth is revealed to us, all that has been imposed upon us by human belief will drop away, and as soon as we begin to perceive our true nature and identity, it will not take long to become accustomed to the atmosphere of Spirit, which is our original abiding place.

Bit by bit, as we pursue the spiritual path, as we realize that our real heritage and identity are in God and that we are of the household of God, living in fellowship with the children of God, we begin to lose pride in our family name and heritage, and inwardly, we may take on a new name, indicating that we have come to a place where we identify ourselves with our Source.

We are all one. The only difference is in the same way that an apple is different from a peach or a pear or a plum—different in individuality, but the same in life, with the same Source, the same feeding, the same protection, the same government. And then I begin to see that as long as I am one with my Source, I am one with each one of you. We are all one with each other because the same life flow that is mine is the same life flow that is yours.

I begin to perceive why the Master said, "Inasmuch as ye have done it unto to the least of these my brethren, ye have done it unto me."[23] I can commence to see that if it were at all possible for me to damage any one of you, that since the life of us is one, I would be damaging myself. If I could benefit any one of you, I really would be benefiting myself, because, in this whole tree of life, there is only one Self flowing out through the vine as our individual being.

Now, to learn this, to read this, to hear this is one thing. Even to have a feeling within us, "Yes, this must be true," is another thing. The third thing is to make it demonstrable in our experience. The only way in which anything can enter your life's experience is through your consciousness. Nothing can come into your experience except through your consciousness.

PART 2

THE GARDEN OF EDEN

III

HEAVEN IS EARTH
SPIRITUALLY UNDERSTOOD

"MY KINGDOM"[1] is not up in heaven, and "this world" is not down on earth. But whether or not we are living in this world or heaven, in My kingdom, depends not on going someplace at some time, but on the degree of spiritual discernment that is developed within us. It determines the degree of heaven we experience; the lack of it determines the degree of hell we experience. "I and my Father are one"[2] is a universal relationship, but certainly, you would never believe it looking at the human race because it isn't the human race that is one with God, or else it would be God-governed and God-maintained. It is the Son of God that is raised up in you through spiritual discernment.

Spiritual discernment deprives us of a great deal of emotion and sensuality, and sometimes we wonder if there is anything to take the place of these good emotions or nice sensuality, but indeed, there is. With the spiritual capacity comes an awareness of God's universe, God's man, and God's body, which far transcends any human sense of joy or beauty that the mind can know.

"Leave thy nets"[3]; leave the physical sense of universe— sun, moon, stars, mountains, seas, and human bodies—and come unto Me. See as *I* see, hear as *I* hear, discern as *I* do, the spiritual nature of this universe, and then find that heaven is established on earth.

Responding and Reacting to the World

Spiritually, the world is embodied in us, within our consciousness. To be able to experience this, you must understand what that means. We live in a world of mountains and valleys, streams and rivers and oceans, suns, moons, and stars; we live in a world of warmth and ice, but we react to this world from our state of consciousness. Actually, there is no good or evil in the world. The world is a mountain, a valley, a river, an ocean, a tree, a sun, moon, a star, but it is not good, it is not bad, nor any degree in between.

When we, who live here, say how wonderful is life in these Hawaiian Islands with its beauty, climate, foliage, ocean, mountains, we are investing these islands with the qualities of good. There are those in other states who would not find this quite so good because they would miss the snow, and the ice, and the cool air—snappy, chilly evenings—and the brisk mornings. All of this constitutes living not only in this world but of this world. We are responding to appearances; we are responding to beliefs.

In other words, we respond to a universal belief, even when there is no truth in it. And so it is that we have found beauty in things, persons, circumstances where there was no beauty, and we have found ugliness where there was no ugliness, all because we were responding to universal belief.

Now, as you approach the spiritual life, you are told to "Judge not after appearances,"[4] and this doesn't mean that you are merely to judge not after negative appearances, but judge not after any appearances. Even the Master says, "Why callest thou me good?"[5] Don't even respond to the appearance that seems to say to you, "I am good," for there is but one good. How careful he is to turn us away from every appearance, that we may have the experience.

Now, how do we attain the experience of living in the world but not being of it, not being subject unto it? We do that through an activity of our consciousness. We withdraw good and evil from the appearance. Let us illustrate that and follow along with it.

I must look out here at you and recognize that in the human picture, some are good and some not so good, some well and others not so well, some young and some old. These are all the appearances, and if I am to live in the world and be of it, I must accept you at face value. But to be on the spiritual path, this must change. I must look out here, and I must agree, "There is neither good nor evil before me, neither sickness nor health, neither youth nor age, neither good nor bad, neither sinful nor pure."

Now, I can only do this if I can agree not to judge by appearances, if I can agree even to set my emotions aside so that I do not like the ones I like and not like the ones I may not like. I have to put all of this aside and agree, "God made all that was made, and with my human eyes, I cannot see God's creation." I cannot see you as you are in God— not with my eyes—nor can I know you, nor can I know what you are like or why, in the image and likeness of God. Therefore, I must, whether with my eyes open or closed, I must nevertheless shut out the picture of you as my eyes would see you, as my emotions would like to think of you, and I must turn within and say, "Speak, Lord, thy servant heareth.[6] Reveal to me Thy image and likeness, man in the image and likeness of God, the manifestation of God's own being."

And you see what I am doing: In the moment that I have agreed not to judge by appearances, I have set something within me toward the development of a soul faculty, a spiritual discernment. I have established an agreement within myself that what I see, hear, taste, touch, and smell have nothing to do with you as you are, and I have agreed within myself, then, that I cannot judge you by any human standard of the five physical senses. Therefore, I must wait on God; I must wait for spiritual discernment to reveal to me, you as you are.

Remember that you have opportunities for this all day long and all night long. Firstly, it is necessary that you come to know the members of your own family as they are, rather than as they appear to be. You will never be entirely satisfied with them as they appear humanly to be. And true happiness can only come in discerning the real nature of that which is hidden from view.

Then, as you practice this, you discover some are coming to you and asking for help and prayer. You will find that this is the mode, this is the means, this is the way of spiritual prayer or treatment or healing consciousness: agreeing first that this human being is not what they appear to be, that I cannot see, hear, taste, touch or smell them as they are in God's image and likeness, and that I cannot judge them by any standard of the human mind. Therefore, I must wait for a spiritual faculty to develop within me that enables me to discern man, or this particular man, woman, or child, in the image and likeness of God.

To attain this consciousness, I must do this with cats and dogs, trees, mountains, and oceans. I must stop loving oceans because my nature happens to be one that loves to be close to the sea; I must stop loving mountains because my nature might be one that responds to being in the high places, and I must begin to discern the mountains and the seas from God's standpoint.

God did not make a mountain for some people to like and some not to like. God did not make a sea to be wonderful to some and destructive to others. God did not make trees to bless some and not others. All that God made is good.

Now, there are many who do not like cats and many who do not like dogs and some who do not like animals at all and certainly many who fear reptiles and beasts. But on this spiritual path, you cannot remain in the world and of it. You must remain "in it but not of it,"[7] and the way is to turn your attention to the reptiles or the beasts. You don't have to go out into the mountains and face them physically, but right where you are, face this world, the part of it that you do like and the part that you do not like, and agree, "There is more to you than the eye beholds. Until I have developed the capacity of spiritual discernment, I will not know man as he is in God, and I will not know this world as it is in God, and therefore, I will never know what it is to live in the Garden of Eden."

Eden: The State of Divine Consciousness

The Garden of Eden does not exist in time. It does not even exist in the future for you, and the Garden of Eden does not exist in space. There is no place where you will find it, even those spots on the face of the globe where it is claimed that the Garden of Eden once was.

No, it never was there, because the Garden of Eden is a state of divine Consciousness, and we live in it now and here in proportion as we can discern man, the nature and character of man as he is in the image and likeness of God, as we can discern the mountains and the valleys and the trees, the streams and the oceans as they are as God's creation. God's creation is spiritual, and therefore, as this inner faculty is developed, you will begin to see spiritually, hear spiritually, and know spiritually, all of which constitutes discernment.

"Hast thou been with me so long, Philip, and hast not known?[8] Whom do men say that I am? Who sayest thou that I am?"[9] Do you see how all of this goes back to the Master? Are you seeing Jesus as a man? Are you seeing me as a man? Are you seeing your wife or husband or child as man, woman, or child? Or, do you have eyes that really see? Do you have ears that really hear? Do you have a power of discernment that transcends the five physical senses?

Now on this point hinges the entire spiritual life, and on this point hinges spiritual healing. With the five physical senses, with the human mind, we would be more than foolish if we said there is no sin or disease or death in the world, or if we were to say there is no lack or limitation or no stupidity. But once spiritual discernment has been attained, even in a small measure, we begin to perceive God's creation right there where mortality appears to be, and this constitutes the healing consciousness. All there is to a student who is doing spiritual healing work and the rest of the world is that those doing the healing work have attained enough of spiritual discernment to see through the appearance to the world, the man, the law of God's creating.

You see, then, that we build this power of spiritual discernment, this capacity of spiritual discernment, in the moment that we agree that God's universe is wholly good, God's universe is wholly spiritual.

You know that Christhood, the full Christhood, is the measure of your being. You also know that you cannot claim to have fully attained, but since you know the goal and since you know that the only way of attainment is the further development of this spiritual capacity of discernment, you know that it involves practice, practice, practice constantly.

Fortunately, we have the opportunity throughout our waking hours, and in a measure carrying it over into our sleeping hours, we have the capacity to consciously remember, every time that we invest anything with a quality of good, to immediately withdraw it and say, "No, no. Father, reveal to me the true quality." And every time we invest anything or anybody with any quality of humanhood, positive or negative, withdraw it and turn to this power of discernment that is within you and ask for light, and then you will receive light on its true nature. As this develops, by beholding more and more of Christhood, we become more and more of Christ.

In The Infinite Way, this is called the middle path: neither good humanhood nor bad humanhood, but spirituality; neither healthy humanhood nor sickly humanhood, but spirituality; neither young age nor old age nor middle age, but eternal age, immortality. In other words, we are withdrawing the qualities of good and evil, up and down, sick and well, rich and poor. We are withdrawing all of this and then letting spiritual discernment reveal to us the spiritual nature of creation.

Departure from Eden:
No Longer God-Governed

God formed this world of the Consciousness which God is: all of this world—the animal, vegetable, mineral, and hu-

man world. But since God is infinite, God could only have
evolved this world out of Himself, out of the Consciousness
which God is.

Therefore, we have existed since the beginning. We were
never born; we will never die because God evolved us of His
consciousness. And "that which God hath joined can never
be put asunder.[10] I and the Father are one," made so not by
me, but by God. God established that relationship in the
beginning: that God, the Father, and God, the Son, is One,
and that Oneness endures forever.

Now at some time, something happened. It is described
in Scripture as the Adamic experience, that is, Adam and
Eve, symbolic figures, not actual. Adam and Eve accepted
a belief in two powers: a power of good and a power of
evil. And by accepting that belief, they were thrown out of
the Garden of Eden. Adam and Eve represent mortal man,
the human being, the human race; therefore, it means that
because of the universal acceptance of two powers—good
power and evil power—we have become separated from
our Source: Eden, heaven, God-consciousness, the Father's
house. Nothing separates us from infinite divine harmony
except a universal belief in two powers, which we naturally
have accepted by having been born.

In the moment that sense of separation sprang up, when
Adam and Eve were cast out of the Garden of Eden, we find
a mortal concept being entertained in the form of two sons.
These two sons are not sons of God; they are the mortal
concepts of the human race—one good and one evil.

From that time on, the human race has been a branch of
a tree that is cut off, withers, and dies. From that time on,
the human race has had no contact with God. And in case
you doubt it, refer to the New Testament, where Paul makes

it very clear that "the natural man receiveth not the things of God."[11] The natural man cannot understand or know the things of God or experience the things of God, for these are spiritually discerned. The natural man is "not under the law of God, neither indeed can be."[12] All of this is summed up by the Master: "if you are not abiding in God and God is not abiding in you, you are a branch of a tree that is cut off and withers and dies."[13] And this is the human race.

Now, just think that we have a world of more than three billion people on the face of the earth of whom it can be said, they are the branch that is cut off, and they're not under the law of God. They're not being blessed by God; they are not receiving the grace of God.

It isn't difficult for you to understand because, in this particular age, you can look out at the people of China and other parts of Asia, India, Russia, and you can see how desolate the scene is. And if you have discernment, you could look right out over the United States and see the barrenness in the souls of most of its people. You could look into its bookshops and see the fewness of the spiritual books available, or that are even called for. You could see that with all of the great scientific and industrial development, there has been a lack of spiritual development. And then you would know what it means to be the natural man. You can see in the relationships between management and labor how devoid of God that relationship has been, to what great extent there has been "man's inhumanity to man."[14] You can see in the wide separation of government and those governed, how desolate that relationship is, how far apart we are as a nation of people from any interest in, or sympathy with, those who govern and vice versa. All of this is for one reason: Until the Spirit of God is admitted into our consciousness, we are under the law of self-protection, self-justification—the law of self-preservation being the first law of human nature. But as the Spirit of God comes into our soul, we come into the ability to love our neighbor, near neighbor and far neighbor, as ourselves.

The Return to Eden: Spiritual Sonship

The goal of our work in The Infinite Way is the goal of realization of our true identity, the goal of realization of the name and nature of God, and the attainment of our conscious union with God. It is the goal. One of the first lessons has to do with how—how do we reach this goal? How do we attain it?

It is when we can understand and emulate the Master: "I of my own self am nothing; I of my own self can do nothing. If I speak of myself, I bear witness to a lie.[15] It is the Father within me that doeth the works.[16] Why callest thou me good? There is but one good, the Father within me."[17] And this state of humility opens our consciousness to receive God's grace. It is the nothingization of personal selfhood and the opening of oneself to the realization of our true identity—and remember that our true identity is spiritual sonship. We are Sons of God "if so be the Spirit of God dwell in us."[18] If we realize that whatever qualities we have, these are the qualities of God; this represents our divine sonship.

God can only be realized by impartation within us. In other words, when the revelation comes, it comes within our being, and it comes through the "still small voice. God is not in the whirlwind; God is not out there in the storm."[19] God is not in a problem. God is in the "still small voice," and the reason so many drop away is they find it impossible to be still.

When you develop the listening ear, when you develop an inner stillness that always has with it the ability—even while conducting your business outwardly—the ability, inwardly, to be still and hear, receive these impartations, you will then begin to hear the Voice. But it is just like a radio station that's on the air twenty-four hours a day. It is always speaking. If your set is turned off, you are not hearing. As human beings, we are cut off. Let me quote from the Master on this, from the 15th chapter of John:

> I am the true vine, and my Father is the husbandman.
>
> Every branch in me that beareth not fruit he taketh away: and every branch that beareth fruit, he purgeth it, that it may bring forth more fruit.
>
> Abide in me, and I in you. As the branch cannot bear fruit of itself, except it abide in the vine; no more can ye, except ye abide in me.
>
> I am the vine; ye are the branches: He that abideth in me, and I in him, the same bringeth forth much fruit: for without me ye can do nothing.
>
> If a man abides not in me, he is cast forth as a branch, and is withered; and men gather them, and cast them into the fire, and they are burned.
>
> John 15: 1-6

Now can you imagine the human race—how much time it has spent from birth, turning within and recognizing that the Christ indwelleth? Can you imagine how much time the human race has spent from birth turning within and realizing, "Thou art the vine and I am the branch, and I am fed by Thee"? I am not dependent on my parents. I am not dependent on my investments. I am not dependent on my children. I am dependent on my contact, on my oneness with the vine, which is within me.

Can you imagine the human race spending time thinking of this and yet reading this Sunday after Sunday after Sunday or hearing it time after time after time—everyone in the world practically owning a book with it in it, and how many living it? And yet, to be the child of God, to be fed from within, to be at one with our Source, there is the teaching. You must abide in Me and let Me abide in you. It means you must not only recognize that *I* abide in you, you must continuously turn within and instead of the first thought being "Who is going to give me this?" or "Through whom am I going to get that?" or "How am I to achieve this?" the first thought should be "My oneness with my Source provides it." Because I am the branch that is one with the vine, all must flow to me from within.

Just think now of the fruit tree, the barren branch looking over at another tree and saying, "Can you lend me some fruit?" That's what we're doing—"Can you lend me?" or "Can you give me?" And in desperate times, we even want to steal it. And yet the fruitage of our lives must come forth from within our being because it has been provided so.

We are the branch, the Son of God, or Christ within us, the indwelling Son of God, or Christ is the vine, and our fruitage must come forth from there. And so it is that you can understand how still, the degree of stillness we must ultimately demonstrate if we are to hear that "still small voice" say,

> *Be still. Be still. Fear not. I am with you. I will never leave thee; I will never forsake thee. I am thy fruit. Not*

the banker, not your friend, not your relative—I am the fruit. Abide in Me, and in due season the fruitage will come forth.

It isn't that there isn't a God. It is that we are cut off from God. It need not be, and Paul reveals that "if so be the Spirit of God dwell in you, then do you become the child of God; then are you heir of God, joint-heir to all that God has."[20] Ah, here we begin to penetrate the mystery of life. It is possible for any human being to give up his status of human being and become a child of God. It is possible to give up our status of being a branch of a tree that is cut off and withers and dies and become an heir of God, living under the government of God, under the grace of God.

Joint-Heir to All of Heaven

Human beings are the unillumined: they are born and brought up in ignorance of their true identity, in ignorance of that indwelling Something, and uninstructed by the divine Master. It is the human race as we know it; these are the people we read about in the newspapers—those in prison, in the prison of lack, sin, and disease, in the prison of political and ecclesiastical slavery, and scholastic ignorance—these are the unillumined, the earthbound.

From the beginning of all revelation, it has been pointed out that this need not be, that at any time we can turn within and begin our ascent out of the tomb of our darkness, out of prison into the light, out of ignorance into understanding. The unillumined can become the illumined. The man living in darkness can become the light of the world. The man living in sin, disease, and poverty can become the Son of God, and thereby an heir of God, joint-heir to all of heaven.

Only when we begin to understand that there is an inner kingdom, only when we can agree that there is a realm of knowledge unknown to "the natural man," only then can we begin our search. We must arrive at the point where we are able to perceive what the Master meant when he said, "My kingdom is not of this world...[21] Put up again thy sword into his place: for all they that take the swords shall perish with the sword."[22]

The unillumined, unaware that they can have recourse to an inner infinite Source, have to endure all the limitations of this world. The illumined, who have touched the infinite Divinity at the center of their being, are never limited to time, space, place, or amount. There is no limitation when we realize that the whole kingdom of God is locked up within us. It does not have to be attained; we do not have to go to God for it. We have to loose it from within ourselves.

God, in the beginning, planted Himself in us and breathed into us His breath of life. He did not breathe into us human life: He breathed into us His life. God did not give us a limited soul, but the soul of God—infinite, eternal, and immortal—if we but go to that center.

Your Externalized
State of Consciousness

Did not God in Genesis give man dominion? Therefore, man must have all the God-power there is, not of himself, but by his oneness with the Father, heir of God to all of the heavenly power. Therefore, there is no power in heaven or on earth greater than *I Am*. Then you can rest and go to sleep if you like. But *I* will never go to sleep, "for I never slumber nor sleep."[23]

Then, in your meditation, take the principle of the nature of God and prayer, and rehearse in your meditation the truth that *I* is "closer to you than breathing"[24]; that the nature of that *I* is omniscience, omnipotence, omnipresence, and therefore all pictures of sense are illusory pictures, made up of the nature of mirage. Whence came that mirage? From a universal belief in two powers, the Adamic experience that expelled Adam and Eve from the Garden of Eden, accepting two powers, good and evil whereas there is neither good nor evil. There is only spiritual harmony, spiritual wholeness, spiritual completeness.

There is nothing external to you that is good or evil. Whatever of good or evil it has, you, by accepting universal beliefs, have given it, and you can at any time withdraw it. There is nothing out here that is good or evil, but thinking makes it so. Not your particular thinking—it's a universal belief that we accept. You must nullify that universal belief that there is power in something or someone out here and must realize that all power is vested in the *I* that I am, in the spiritual Presence within me. Then, everything out here will reflect back to us good.

You have the example that there is neither good nor evil in this room. Whatever there is in this room, we have brought here in our consciousness. If there is love, if there is love thy neighbor, if there is sharing, if there is forgiving, we brought it here; we did not find it here in the room. The room was empty.

If any individual comes in here with hate, animosity, jealousy, and all the human attributes, they're very apt to lose it by virtue of this united consciousness of love. But if not, and they go out and say, "There was no love in that room," it was because they didn't bring the love in with them. They probably couldn't find here what they didn't bring here. There is only what we have brought to this room.

So, regardless of where we go, we carry with us our world internally, and we externalize it. So if I carry within me the "praying without ceasing"[25] attitude and atmosphere, which is abiding in this Spirit of God within me as the all-power, the all-presence, the all-wisdom, that is what I am projecting, and that is what you are feeling. Knowing this, it becomes my responsibility not to allow anything else to enter my consciousness. It is a discipline.

That is why the Master said "the way is strait and narrow, and few there be that enter."[26] It is a discipline, and there are few that enter because there are so few willing to take a few years of discipline until they have rebuilt their consciousness, until they have died to their human sense of good and evil and been reborn into the consciousness of oneness.

It becomes necessary for us to work with whichever of these principles strikes us forcibly. All of us cannot work with all of these principles. Some of us can only work with one of them for a long, long time. Others may be able to work with two or three. But eventually, we have to work with all of them, and in doing this we are dying daily, and we are being reborn. But do not expect any greater blessings in your outer world than the measure of your transformation of consciousness because it cannot be. You cannot have anything on the moving picture screen except that which is on the film, and so you cannot externalize in your life anything other than your state of consciousness. No one has dominion in his own life until he comes to an understanding of the fact that he embraces within his own consciousness all that he is to externalize in his experience.

There is the story told of a man getting on a train at a certain stop and seating himself beside a minister on the train. As they came near the next station, it was evident that the minister was going to get off, and the man said, "Oh, do you live here in this town?" "Yes, I do." "Well, I'm thinking of coming here to live. What kind of town is this? What kind of people do you have here?"

The minister looked at him and said, "Why what kind of people do you have in the town you have lived in?" "Ah," he said, "they're mean. They're bad. They're ugly." "That's just exactly what you're going to meet in this town."

Of course, you're bringing them here. You're bringing them here. You can't find, in this town, anything that you don't bring here. If you are to find love, you must bring love. If you are to find friendship, you must bring friendship. If you are to find honesty, you must bring the honesty. It isn't here. It isn't out in the air. It isn't in the air in this room or out on the street or in the building. Whatever qualities there are, these qualities are to be found in consciousness, your consciousness or mine.

What you and I are receiving as benefits from our study and practice of the Infinite Way is far less important than what the message is doing in the raising up of the entire world. It must be remembered that there is no Infinite Way separate and apart from your consciousness and mine. There is no Infinite Way hanging in space. Whatever Infinite Way there is on earth is what is active in consciousness, and unless Infinite Way principles find activity and expression in individual consciousness, they will not be expressed in the world. Therefore, each of us has the responsibility to live these principles.

PART 3

INTO A FAR COUNTRY

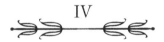

IV

WHEN WE ARE
TEMPTED BY GOOD AND EVIL

I HAVE KNOWN FROM the beginning that we were dealing with a spiritual universe and that the evil in it wasn't
real, but I never knew why, nor did I know how we came into
this state of being out of Eden until the revelation came.

The revelation came in those passages where God said,
"Who told you that you were naked?"[1] And then I knew that
something was wrong. Then, when it said, "the knowledge
of good and evil,"[2] and Adam and Eve were thrown out of
Eden—that gave me the whole secret.

Eden represents our spiritual domain. Eden represents
the state of harmony or heaven. Eden represents our
immortality, our state of divine being. What threw us out
of that into what the Master called "this world"?[3] There it
is, as plain as anyone can read: the knowledge of good and
evil—that's what did it.

For weeks I didn't get over the shaking that I got from
the intensity of that revelation—that the cause of all the
trouble on the face of the earth is the belief in good and
evil; nobody can stay in the Garden of Eden, of harmony, of
perfection, while they are accepting in their mind the belief
of good and evil.

But everybody can go back into Eden and be pure, and have lives by grace, not by the sweat of the brow; by grace, by the gift of God, by giving up the belief of good and evil; by being willing to concede that there's no good man on earth and no bad one; no good woman on earth, no bad one; no good child on earth, no bad one. There is neither good nor bad. Thinking would make it so.

Yes, you can decide that this is good, and the other one can decide that is good. You can decide this is evil, and the other one can decide that is evil. But you withdraw your estimate, your opinion, your concept, and declare that "in all of heaven and earth, nothing is good or evil—only God Itself, the Invisible, is the all-good; nothing visible, nothing that you can see, hear, taste, touch, or smell is good, nor is it evil, nor has it any qualities like such." Only the Invisible is good, and that Invisible permeates the visible and gives it its qualities.

In other words, to say that a rose garden is beautiful is true. To say "it's good" is untrue, because the good is the invisible Presence and Power that formed it. That's the good and the visible merely reflects that goodness, but it's the invisible nature that is the good.

Inside of thirty days, your whole life could change if you have the strength to withhold all judgments as to good and evil and realize,

I will not know good or evil; I will know only God as good.

And then let this world be whatever it wants to be or appears to be, to the world. But for you, never again judge good or evil.

Again, is it not written, "There is nothing good or bad, but thinking makes it so"[4]—our accepting two powers? Is not this the reason that Adam and Eve are expelled from the Garden of Eden—because they have eaten of the tree of the knowledge of good and evil, they have accepted mentally two powers? Have we not suffered in this whole generation because we have been afraid of certain government leaders, certain political powers, certain political forces without having learned from the Master this great truth: "Thou couldest have no power over me"[5]—temporality, temporal powers—"Thou couldest have no power except it were given thee of God" because God is infinite? God is the only power. God is the all-power.

We begin a daily practice every time some person seems to dominate us, whether in the family life or the community life, national or international. We go through a daily practice of,

> *Aha! I am not to be fooled by appearances. There is no power given unto man. All power is in God. All power is in the Spirit. All power is in the Invisible. And those who show forth good are showing forth the presence and power of God. Those who are showing forth evil are showing forth the arm of flesh, or nothingness, and its power over us has been our fear of it, our acceptance of two powers, our lack of understanding that God is the only power.*

You would be surprised what happens in your individual experience for a week or two if you were to practice the principle: "There is no good or evil." You'd find yourself pretty nearly torn apart if you caught the awareness of what you are doing. For a week or two, you would not be able to live your normal, natural life. You'd be upset, and you'd be in conflict with yourself and with every appearance that you meet, because at this moment, as you look out, you are well satisfied with some things and much displeased with others. There are some things that you like so well you wish you had more of them, and some things you dislike so much you wish you could get rid of them. And that's what's causing trouble, and for a week or two it'll cause a little more trouble when you try to change that situation and come to the realization, "There is nothing good or evil."

Therefore, there is nothing for me to desire, nothing for me to change in myself or another. There is neither good nor evil. The difficulty comes when we behold those around us and behold those qualities that we would like to see changed in them and realize that we have to tighten up our teeth and grit them a bit and say, "No, no, it's neither good nor evil."

Judging Good or Evil

Close your eyes and think of any person you like or any condition or any condition of any person. Let us look right at it, and declare within ourselves, "This is neither good nor evil; this has no qualities within itself of either good or evil. Now, if this is a good person or good condition, then I have conditioned my mind and labeled this person good or evil, or this person or condition good. If I declare this person or this condition evil, who said so?"

God said to Adam, "Who toldest thou that thou was naked?" Where did this information arise? A moment ago, there was neither good nor evil; a moment ago, you were naked and didn't mind it. Now, why do you mind it? Something has conditioned your mind, and you see yourself one way as good and another way as evil. But the condition in and of itself is neither good nor evil; it is just a state of being.

Try for a moment to think of a painting or a piece of music or statuary, and see whether it is good or not good. And then ask yourself, "Would the whole world agree with me?" Of course not. That which you are seeing as good, someone else is seeing as not good or less good or not at all good or positively evil. Look at people, and ask yourself if everyone agrees with your estimate of them. And you'll find that their mothers think far differently about them than their enemies. Then, is the quality of good in the person or in the concept of that person?

As we know through our spiritual revelation, the Master says, "Why callest thou me good? There is but one good, the Father in heaven,"[6] showing that actually the Master wasn't good; he was an instrument through which good manifested. Paul says, "I am not a sinner, yet I feel within myself a sense of sin."[7] So we know that evil is not personal; it is not a man being evil, even though momentarily a man may be the instrument through which evil manifests. The point I'm trying to bring to your attention—and you're looking now in your silence, you're looking at some man or woman—is this: Remember that man or woman is neither good nor evil regardless of the judgment of your physical senses. They are not good, and they are not evil: they are person.

> And the scribes and Pharisees brought unto him a woman taken in adultery; and when they had set her in the midst,
>
> They say unto him, Master, this woman was taken in adultery, in the very act.
>
> Now Moses in the law commanded us, that such should be stoned: but what sayest thou?
>
> This they said, tempting him, that they might have to accuse him. But Jesus stooped down, and with his finger wrote on the ground, as though he heard them not.

So when they continued asking him, he lifted up himself, and said unto them, He that is without sin among you, let him first cast a stone at her.

And again he stooped down, and wrote on the ground.

And they which heard it, being convicted by their own conscience, went out one by one, beginning at the eldest, even unto the last: and Jesus was left alone, and the woman standing in the midst.

When Jesus had lifted up himself, and saw none but the woman, he said unto her, Woman, where are those thine accusers? hath no man condemned thee?

She said, No man, Lord. And Jesus said unto her, Neither do I condemn thee: go, and sin no more.

John 8: 3-11

How can we possibly accept a teaching that reveals God as the life of all being, as the creative principle of all being, and then designate some good and some bad? The woman taken in adultery was not labeled by the Master. "Woman, where are those thine accusers? Neither do I condemn thee." To the thief on the cross, he said, "Today shalt thou be with me in paradise,"[8] and to the man born blind, "Neither hath this man sinned nor his parents."[9]

Do you begin to understand the necessity of foregoing all censure, all condemnation based on appearances? Every spiritual teaching and revelation from 1500 B.C. is based upon the postulates "Love thy neighbor as thyself"[10] and "Do unto others as you would have others do unto you."[11] Prayer is our contact with God, and we have no contact with God unless we love our neighbors as ourselves; this will, of course, deprive us of many of our social and political discussions, for we will no longer be able to blame our families or friends, our business associates, or the heads of our government for our troubles, circumstances, and depressions.

It calls for discipline on the part of each one of us, and it calls for something more: it calls for a deep and great love of God. No one can come into the holy atmosphere of God voicing criticism, judgment, or condemnation of his fellow man. "Therefore if thou bring thy gift to the altar, and there rememberest that thy brother hath ought against thee; leave there thy gift before the altar, and go thy way; first be reconciled to thy brother, and then come and offer thy gift."[12]

There can be no spiritual demonstration while we hold to human opinions of good and evil. When we look at the world with no opinions, judgments, or labels—not even good ones—but with the realization that God *is*, we set up a sort of a vacuum within. Into that vacuum surges the spiritual wisdom defining and evaluating that which is before us, and this we find to be entirely different from our human estimate.

This is what makes the spiritual path different and difficult. It requires a whole transformation of consciousness, what in Paul is called "dying daily"[13] and being reborn, what the Master calls "dying"—dying and being reborn of the Spirit. It is a death to our human consciousness, that consciousness which is made up of both good and evil, that consciousness in which we praise people who do good and condemn those who do evil, whereas we have no right to do either.

When you reach the point where you can understand that all human conditions of whatever name or nature exist but as a belief in the human mind, a belief that resulted in man's expulsion from the Garden of Eden, and when you become convinced in your innermost heart that because God is infinite, there are no pairs of opposites, you can say with the Master, "I have overcome the world." [14] Then, you are back in the kingdom of heaven.

As we approach the healing work, we should have in our consciousness no awareness of evil to be removed or risen above, but because so much of humanhood remains in most of us, we still recognize that there is before us the appearance of evil in the form of sin, disease, death, lack, and limitation. And as long as we are faced with such appearances, we cannot be absolute and, ostrich-like, ignore the appearance, repeating over and over again, "Oh, God is all; there is no error." That is useless and foolish. We should not do that. We should let God say it to us, and when we hear the "still small voice" or when we feel that stirring within us, we may be assured that whatever appearance of sin, disease, death, lack, or limitation is before us will melt away. But do not think that you humanly can ever be so wise as to bring this about.

Because you know the words and can say orally or silently, "There is neither good nor evil," do not believe that their repetition will work miracles in your life because it will not. You have to live with this truth until you can demonstrate it; you have to prove it over and over again within yourself. Moreover, never forget that if you are tempted to tell this to any man before it becomes so evident that the world sees it in you, you will lose what you have received, and what is more, you may lose even the possibility of demonstrating it in this incarnation because no one can trifle with the word of God, no one can boast with it and play with it and think that he can retain it.

You can only prove this principle in the degree that you hug it tightly within yourself; keep it sacred and keep it secret, but use it. Use it morning, noon, and night with every bit of error that confronts you, whether in the newspaper, on the radio, in your family, or on the street.

Wherever and whenever you are faced with error, turn and ask yourself, "Can this make me believe in good or evil? Can I be made to accept two powers?" If you can do that, you will refrain from accepting or judging by appearances, and you will not be tempted to try to heal somebody or something, but you will stay within yourself and judge righteous judgment, stay within the Garden of Eden which represents your spiritual domain, the state of divine harmony.

Spiritual healing cannot take place on the human plane. It can take place only when you have stopped thinking of the person, and the disease and the condition and the belief and the claim and have returned to Eden where there is only God, Spirit, wholeness and completeness. Nobody can ever be a spiritual healer who works from the standpoint of effect or who prays from the standpoint of trying to correct something in the Adam-world because if he succeeded, he would but have exchanged an unpleasant dream for a pleasant one. If he succeeded in improving the human picture, he would only have good materiality instead of bad materiality. He would be no nearer the kingdom of God.

Eventually, you are going to see it's just as much of a sin to believe that there is power in a good thought as to believe that there is power in a bad thought. Why? Because a good thought is just as human as a bad thought, and a human thought isn't power.

In the degree that you lose good and evil, you're no longer human; you're spiritual. That's when you're a healer. You're not as subject to the human errors of life or lacks of life as you were when you were entertaining both good and evil. No. All of a sudden, you have become, to some extent, immune from the claims of the world.

Tempted by "Twoness": Professions of Power

In every walk of life, in every phase of life, you are being confronted with "twoness" or duality, meaning a belief in two powers, two selves, two lives, two strata of existence. And yet the truth is, "Hear, O Israel: the Lord our God, the Lord is one."[15] And that one is Spirit. That one is infinite; that one is Omnipresence, Omniscience, Omnipotence, and besides this one, God, infinite good, there is none besides.

Now, this belief in two powers, as I have said, because of its universal nature, is so powerful that it acts hypnotically, and Paul, in summing up the nature of the one evil that confronts all of us, called it "the carnal mind."[16] And we sometimes use that term, "the carnal mind." And by that term, we mean this universal belief in two powers. We don't mean that there is an actual mind called a carnal mind; there is no such thing. But just to shorten this universal belief in two powers, we call it "the carnal mind." It can be called "mortal mind"; it means the same thing. It means a universal belief in a power which isn't a power.

In other words, when you see mortal mind or carnal mind, not as an enemy, not as something to be overcome or destroyed, not as something you have to protect yourself from, but when you see carnal mind or mortal mind as a universal belief in two powers, and you don't believe in two powers, you have already overcome the carnal mind and its effects, at least in the degree of your realization.

Not many people on the face of the globe dispute the fact of God today, but they may well dispute God's presence and God's power in human affairs because, looking out upon this world, there is truly very little evidence of it. And it is only as individuals come in their own experience to an actual God-realization that they know without doubt that God does operate in human affairs.

In starting our work, I would like to say at the very beginning that there is one part of it, one feature of it, that must be thoroughly understood before you undertake in any way to bring God into active expression in your affairs. Now, watch this carefully for the simple reason that you will not meet very often with this principle in the teachings of this world.

Ordinarily we think of the evils of the world, and then if we think of God, we think of God as overcoming those evils, as God destroying the errors of the world or God reforming the evil ones of the world, and I give it to you as a principle that this is incorrect. There is no such thing in all the world as God overcoming or destroying evil. There is no such thing in all the world as truth overcoming error. There is no such thing in all the world as God being a power over evils: evil persons or evil conditions or evil circumstances.

In other words, God is not a power that can be used over other powers. God is not a power of good overcoming powers of evil, and the reason is God is infinite; good is infinite, and that which the world has been calling "powers" really are not powers at all. The only reason that we have had occasion to fight and battle these discords is that we, ourselves, have made enemies of that which in and of itself has no power.

Now, in the same way this principle is being brought into capital and labor relations, even into politics. Once you enter the state of consciousness in which you recognize God as the only power, you no longer battle evil men and women. You no longer battle evil causes. You no longer battle the so-called errors of the world. You learn to "stand still and see the salvation of the Lord"[17]—of the law, of the one law. You stand still and watch the one law in operation. You can stand as defenseless as Daniel before the lion, or you can stand as defenseless as Jesus Christ before Pilate, saying, "Thou couldest have no power over me." Pilate, the greatest temporal power in the world, and Jesus says, "Thou couldest have no power over me unless it came from the Father in heaven."

Or you could be out there with young David, young David going out to Goliath and finding that his friends wanted to laden him down with armor, armor—steel armor, iron armor, whatever it was they used for heavy armor in those days—and he says, "No, no, no; take that off me. I require no armor. I am going out there in the name of the Lord God Almighty."[18] In other words, "I'm going out there in the understanding of God as the only might."

Now, if God is the only might, what power has Goliath? What power has the sword of Goliath? What power have infection or contagion? What power have the evil plots and plans of men in the face of an individual who is alert to the real nature of God? The secret of the world's failure for these thousands of years has been that it has not known the nature of God, and therefore it has prayed to God to "do

something to my enemy"—to remove them, to overcome
them, to destroy them—and there's no God to listen to such
prayers. There's no God to answer such prayers.

Why? Because in the entire realm of the real, there has
never been a power endowed with power against God.
Since God is supreme, infinite, omnipresent, final, what
would empower a devil? What would empower a power
apart from God? Whence would this power be derived if
you posit God as Infinity, as infinite Being, as One. "Hear,
O Israel, the Lord our God, the Lord is one"—one—one
power, only one.

The minute we withdraw power from men or organiza-
tions and place that power in the Invisible, we automatically
and instantly release ourselves from any evil that man or
conditions can do. We may not instantly release this world
from it, for there is no such thing. We release ourselves first,
and then as we are released, we bring release to those who
come within range of our consciousness.

It is true that "ten righteous men"[19] can save a city. And
it is true that a very small group of individuals who no
longer place their confidence in a political party or political
candidate can change the entire election, the results of the
election. They can take the evil out of an election, and that
doesn't mean they can elect their candidate or their party.
It only means that out of the candidates who are running,
those nearest to the level of spiritual integrity would find
their way elected. And that would be done only by those
who could give up their faith and confidence in any man or
party and realize that all power is in the Invisible. Yes, let
me put it this way: in certain places, votes are controlled by
certain interests.

For instance, in some places, it could be said that the labor vote will control the election in that community; in some other community, it could be that a church would dominate the election. In some other places, it would be that the industrialists have control of the votes in their community. And it is that belief that perpetuates the evils of our world, our political world, because the power is not in an individual or a group. The power is in the Spirit.

Whom Shall I Fear?

This is a quotation from Emerson's essay on "Compensation."

> There is always some leveling circumstance that puts down the overbearing. Though no checks to a new evil appear, the checks exist and will appear. The dice of God are always loaded.

Isn't that tremendous? All you have to do is think back to Caesar, who governed with an iron hand, Genghis Khan, Alexander the Great. In more modern days, the czars of Russia; Hitler, who couldn't be conquered, who carried everything before him. Think: go back in history and find dozens more illustrations, and see if you cannot agree that the dice of God are always loaded. Even though, at the moment, there appears to be nothing to stop the onward march of tyranny, of evil in one form or another, inevitably, these checks appear and become manifest.

Now, Emerson says that there is always some leveling circumstance that puts down the overbearing, but he doesn't name it. He could have named it because he knew it. This circumstance is a law: "as ye sow so shall ye reap[20]; as ye do to another, so it shall be done to you[21]; whatever you bind, will bind you; whatever you set free, will set you free"[22] because all life is lived at the center of our being, and the outward circumstances are governed and controlled by this inner law. The law is very clear. "If you sow to the flesh, you reap corruption; if you sow to the Spirit, you reap life everlasting."[23]

Of course, the question comes up there: What do you mean by sowing to the flesh? What do you mean by sowing to the Spirit? And the answer is this: Do you place the power in flesh or effect, or do you place power in an invisible Source?

In other words, let us look out at world conditions today and ask the question: Do we fear the power of men? Or, if we were going to vote tomorrow, would we be putting our confidence or faith in some man or group of men? And then you'll know whether you are sowing to the flesh.

If you fear "man whose breath is in his nostrils,"[24] you are sowing to the flesh and will reap corruption. On the other hand, if you have any faith or confidence in men, if you have any belief that there is a man or group of men who can save this world, you are equally sowing to the flesh because putting faith in princes has been outmoded for centuries. Putting faith in "man whose breath is in his nostrils" has given us the greatest betrayers of mankind.

Remember that every man who has ever betrayed anyone or anything was first given confidence that put him in the position to do the betraying. You and I have never betrayed a nation, but nobody ever gave us the reins of authority. First, you must empower someone before he can betray the power.

Whether we are thinking in terms of international affairs, or whether we're thinking in terms of our national affairs, it all comes down to: Shall I fear what mortal man can do to me? Shall I fear human circumstances or conditions? Shall I have faith that there is a man or group of men who can save me individually or the world collectively? In either case, the answer is that you would be sowing to the flesh, and you would reap corruption.

You realize that over the centuries, this belief in two powers, the belief in good and the belief in evil, has become strong enough to be hypnotic so that we are all hypnotized with the belief that "this is good and this is bad." We are all hypnotized, to some extent, with the belief that there are good powers and bad powers, spiritual powers and material powers.

To be dehypnotized means merely to come into some measure of agreement that there cannot be God and something besides God. There cannot be Spirit and something unlike or opposite to Spirit. Then, you come to this: whereas in your old belief there was God and devil, or good and evil, and whereas in our early metaphysics we had immortal mind and mortal mind, you now come to the realization that there can be but one mind, one power, one substance, one cause, and as you accept that, your old consciousness becomes spiritualized.

In other words, lack of spiritualization means having two powers; spiritualization means having one power.

Watch Your Response to Good and Evil

If you look around this world, you will see the gross people, the gross materialists, the people that cause you to shudder in their presence. Then, as you look further around, you see the spiritually-minded people, the people in whose presence you feel a sense of Christ envelop you. You must ask yourself, "How come? Why?" And then you'll know that all of us have gone through centuries of development: first, downward from our original Christhood in the Garden of Eden to walking this earth almost as vultures; then, the ascent up to the more highly developed spiritual identity that we are approaching at this moment.

You will see that *I* co-exist with God. From the moment that God is, *I* am. There isn't even the flash, a blink of an eyelash between God and *I*. As a matter of fact, a mystical poet went one step further and said, "Before God was, *I* Am."[25] And that's true because God exists in our consciousness, not as God, but as a concept of God, so what we're talking about as God isn't really God at all, but a concept that has gone through changes over the centuries, and before there was ever a concept called "God," there was *I*. *I* existed before I had a concept of God. *I* existed on this earth, before the word "God" or the belief of one touched my consciousness.

You learn through inner unfoldment that "I and the Father are one."[26] "I and the Father" is a relationship that has existed from the beginning and will exist until the end of the world. Of course, the end of the world means the end of our concept of the world, the end of the concept of our physical world, for the simple reason that when it's all done and we have lost the physical sense of existence, *I* will still be *I*. There's only *I;* there's only one Ego; that has been known since the days of Krishna. Five thousand years ago, it was known there is only one *I*, only one Ego, and *I* am He. *I* am He. Before the days of the Hebrew dispensation, before Moses could say, I AM THAT I AM, the Hindus were saying *I* am He, and *I* am That. Then Moses came with the Hebrew dispensation and brought forth I AM THAT I

AM, and the Master not only repeated that but probably, to our sense, went a step further when he said, "Thou seest me, thou seest the Father that sent me,[27] for I and the Father are one."

If you want to prove that, close your eyes and without egotism, without boasting, just gently, gently, say "*I*," and if you can, don't even say it. Don't say it; just imagine the word "*I.*" *I*—that's me. That's my identity as I have been throughout eternity, and as I will be throughout eternity, but I will only show it forth in the degree that I have no sense of good and evil.

When I can confront any form of sin without horror, without being shocked, without self-righteousness or indignation, when I can look at any form of sin and realize that it can only exist as ignorance, I'm approaching it. When I can stand in the presence of any form of disease and realize it has no power, it's not a thing—I don't even have to get rid of it—then am I approaching, in some degree, the original Christhood in the Garden of Eden where there's no one to declare, "This is good and this is evil; let's get rid of this or rise above that." When we're at that stage, we are touching upon our Christhood.

And so you see that with each of us there is a long road ahead, but we now have a map, some road guides. We know now that we have to take the word "*I*" into our meditation and not do as some do: believe that I, the human being, is God. You won't go far that way, and you are apt to get into serious difficulty. A human being can never be God any more than a human being can be spiritual or under God's law. But you aren't a human being, and you aren't mortal in the degree that this Spirit of God embraces you, that this

Spirit of God enfolds you and you can say "*I*"—but when you say "*I*," don't open your eyes and start hating or fearing or envying or any of that because then you throw the whole business out the window.

When you come out of that *I*, be as pure as you were inside, because inside, in that *I*, you felt no feeling of fear, no feeling of hate, no feeling of jealousy, no feeling at all of conceit. You just felt a self-completeness, a perfection, an inner glow. Now hold that when you come out because the moment you indulge right and wrong, good and evil, and all of these negative qualities of humanity, you are setting yourself back from where you were when you were in that consciousness of the *I*.

The Only Real Peace:
The Kingdom of God Within You

Now, we are going through a period of world history that is fascinating. I wouldn't be surprised that it is more interesting to be alive at this particular time of history than at any other time in world history. It is one of the occasions when the world is going through a major transition. It may be the final transition, that in which material sense is completely overcome, and Christ-consciousness comes upon the world as a universal bestowal. To me, it appears that this is what is happening because as I look out at most of the evils—no, let me say at most of those events that the world calls "evil"—I see them not as evils, but as the breaking up of evils. I see the end of many of the evils of the human mind that existed in the past centuries.

Turn your gaze now to the place where you have already felt that gentle Presence; smile at It. Secretly and sacredly know that It is there and that It is fulfilling its function about the Father's business. This babe was given unto you to be about the Father's business, of "restoring for you the lost years of the locust,"[28] of returning you this last part of the journey back to the Father's house or conscious union with God. It is the function of this babe to reveal that you are living in the midst of Eden, where you will always be tempted with only one temptation. There is only one evil in the Garden of Eden, only one sin: the belief in the power of good and evil.

You, sitting back inside your temple, must be able to look at that tree at all times and resist the temptation to believe in it. You must be able to say,

> *Beautiful as you look, or horrible as you look, I now know there is no truth in you. There is no power of good; there is no power of evil. God in the midst of me is the only power and the only presence.*

Even when you have overcome the three temptations in the wilderness for yourself, you will be tempted with storms at sea; you will be tempted by the adulteress; you will be tempted by the poor; you will be tempted by the disease to accept two powers. That is all that is happening when these temptations come to you. The world will call them cancer and consumption and polio; the world will call them depression and tyrants. The world will call them by many names, but you will sum them all up: "This is a temptation to believe in two powers, and this Christ within me is my assurance that only Christ is power, the Son of God, the Spirit of God in me."

In that same way, we should now look at the world scene and compare it to our own life. If, at any time in our experience, we came to a place and wondered, "Is evil going to win out in this experience with me? Am I going to succumb to death? Am I going to be a permanent invalid? Am I doomed to live in this particular sin for the rest of my days? Is the power of evil greater than whatever the power of God might be, the power of good?" Many have come to situations in their lives of that nature and wondered to what extent evil, error, sin, disease, poverty, and unhappiness were going to remain permanent because evil seemed to be greater than the power of good, even greater than the power of God.

Now, let us turn to the world situation, and as we remember the nature of the evils that face this world today in every country—yours is no exception, ours is no exception—let this same question come to your mind. Is the power of evil abroad in the world going to prove greater than the power of good? Is the power of hate or malice going to prove more powerful than the power of love and brotherhood? Is the desire that you see in a great part of the world today to bring liberation and freedom to the rest of mankind—is this to be thwarted by some evil force or power? Or, is there a power that can dissolve these evils, can change the circumstances of the world, can bring freedom, abundance, harmony, health, peace on earth and goodwill to men? Is there such a thing?

Ask yourself the question: "What is this kingdom of God within me? What is the nature of the kingdom of God within me? What is its function?" In answer to that question lies not only your salvation, your health, your happiness, your peace, and your prosperity, but on this same answer lies the safety and security of the entire world.

If you haven't thought about it, think about it in these coming days as to whether or not you believe that there is a human solution to the world's problems or if you have heard of anyone in this decade who even claims to believe that they have an answer to the world's problems. Then you'll understand why no one, regardless of their position in the government, in politics, in statesmanship, no one claims to have any solution to the major problems of this world. Then you will know why there must be a spiritual solution, or we are coming to the end of another period of human history.

Now, the fact is this: The world is not going to come to an end. Civilization is not going to be destroyed, and harmony is to be restored on earth—not another period of intervals between wars, not another period like 1919 to 1939, but the actual experience of peace on earth. When the final say is said, there will be contracts drawn, there will be treaties signed, but these will not be the reason for peace. These will not even be a factor in the peace. These will only be the result of coming into the actual experience: this kingdom of God is within you.

Return to the Primal Estate: The Father-Consciousness

We always come to that place where, regardless of what we learn, what we are reading or studying, that we have to live the conviction, we have to live the life that is now unfolding to us. There is a period in our experience when we may think of ourselves purely as students or initiates, and during this period, we are learning, yes. We are taking in new principles. We are discarding old religious beliefs and superstitions and theories, doctrines; we are learning not to be dependent on anything that exists in the external realm,

to use everything as it comes along for good but not depend
on it. We are learning that there is only one power and that
it is only a universal belief in two powers that limits us. We
are learning the nature of God. We are learning the nature
of prayer.

For the longest while, we're learning and learning and
learning and unlearning, learning to let go. But then there
comes a period when the thought must come to us: "Now,
what do I do with all of this learning? How do I go further
than learning?" And that, of course, is the beginning of
your real experience—when you start to live what you have
learned.

You have developed something higher than a human
brain and human wisdom. You have developed a spiritual
consciousness, a divine consciousness, which we now call
the "Father-consciousness." You find the same experience in
the story of the prodigal who returned to his father's house.
Now let no one believe for a moment that this means that
he returned to his paternal home; it doesn't mean that at
all. It means that he returned to his primal estate, which
is divine Consciousness. He had fallen from it into human
consciousness and ended up where human consciousness
always must end up because it is dependent on externals.
But he returned to his Father's house, to the "Father-
consciousness," which was his original heritage.

When you awaken to this, you will understand all of
the Bible passages that refer to "Father," and the "Father's
house," or any other reference to "house" that doesn't
mean a residence, and you'll know that "house" means
consciousness. In other words, the Father-consciousness in
you revealed this to you, not the man consciousness, not the
human consciousness, the Father-consciousness of you.

You know when you rightly understand the story of the prodigal son, you will have the secret of life at your fingertips. In the beginning, you are the Father. You are the Father-consciousness. You weren't just a favored son in the beginning. You were a Father, the Father, the Father-consciousness, but you cut yourself off to make yourself a son. It would have been all right to have been a son in the spiritual sense of sonship, as merely an emanation or offspring of God-consciousness, an individualization of God-consciousness, but no, this sense of sonship is separate, and has to receive something of the Father—an inheritance. Now you know there is no such thing in all this world as a son receiving anything from a father, not even a spiritual son receiving anything from a spiritual Father. The spiritual Father is also the spiritual Son: God, the Father, and God, the Son. The Son is just as much God as the Father, and so even as a Son, we are the Father-consciousness, the all-embracing, all-embodying one Consciousness, infinite. By becoming a Son, we do not become less than all, nor do we ever divide our inheritance with our brothers. There is no such thing as division in God.

The Prodigal Son

And he said, A certain man had two sons:

And the younger of them said to his father, Father, give me the portion of goods that falleth to me. And he divided unto them his living.

And not many days after the younger son gathered all together, and took his journey into a far country, and there wasted his substance with riotous living.

And when he had spent all, there arose a mighty famine in that land; and he began to be in want.

And he went and joined himself to a citizen of that country; and he sent him into his fields to feed swine.

And when he came to himself, he said, How many hired servants of my father's have bread enough and to spare, and I perish with hunger!

I will arise and go to my father, and will say unto him, Father, I have sinned against heaven, and before thee,

And am no more worthy to be called thy son: make me as one of thy hired servants.

And he arose, and came to his father. But when he was yet a great way off, his father saw him, and had compassion, and ran, and fell on his neck, and kissed him.

And the son said unto him, Father, I have sinned against heaven, and in thy sight, and am no more worthy to be called thy son.

But the father said to his servants, Bring forth the best robe, and put it on him; and put a ring on his hand, and shoes on his feet:

And bring hither the fatted calf, and kill it; and let us eat, and be merry:

For this my son was dead, and is alive again; he was lost, and is found.

Luke 15:11-24

To be transformed from the man of earth to the man of Christ is not a matter of another world. This is God's universe; right here and now is the Garden of Eden. There could never be a better place than this very world if so be we can withdraw our judgments—our praise and condemnation—of good and evil. This is the world that every visionary has dreamed of attaining, but nobody can attain the Edenic state while he is hypnotized by the knowledge of good and evil. This can come only as the fruitage of relinquishing not only all judgment or condemnation but even all praise. When we are no longer under the hypnotic influence of the pairs of opposites, the world has no power to enslave us. This world is overcome in proportion to our giving up the belief in good and evil, but actually, there is no change in the world itself. It appears to be the same. The great difference is that we do not see it the old way anymore. For us, there is a different light on it; we now have a different perspective, a different outlook.

When we are able to rise above the realm of thought to that high place where we have no opinion whether anything or anybody is good or evil but are willing to be a perfect transparency for the instruction of God, then God speaks in our ear and shows us the spiritual reality which exists right where that "man of flesh who cannot please God"[29] appears to be. But in that instant, when God speaks, the man of flesh is transformed into the Son of God and is immediately returned to the Garden of Eden, where he is now the Son of God living under God's government.

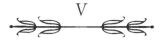

V

WHEN WE
JUDGE BY APPEARANCES

SPIRITUAL DISCERNMENT SEES God appearing as individual being and realizes that every individual has the allness of the Spirit of God, of the grace of God, of the presence of God. It may not appear to be so, judging by appearances, but always remember that what you see, hear, taste, touch, and smell represent the material and limited sense of things. What you discern inwardly will be closer to the truth. It is for this reason that if we would be helpful to the world, we must forget our praying about peace on earth or victories over the enemy or victories of our way of life over another mode of life or victories of our favorite political party over the other. If we would benefit the world, we must pray in spirit and truth, and this means that we must look through the appearances with our powers of spiritual discernment and behold God's government of man and the earth.

Now, as we look at creation, we are not seeing Spirit and Its formations as they are because we are looking out through those eyes of Adam and Eve, who disobeyed the order about good and evil. In other words, we are looking out through eyes that believe that some things are good and some things are evil; therefore, we are not seeing anything as it is.

Nothing are we seeing as it is. And that's why we don't see things alike. That's why one likes this kind of art, and the other likes that kind of art. That is why, in all generations, the great music masters have not been considered musical. It took a hundred years after they were gone before it was acknowledged that their music was true music. In other words, we are creatures of habit and our inhibitions and our background, so if a thing doesn't conform to our idea of beauty, it isn't beautiful. If a thing doesn't conform to our idea of good, it isn't good.

But that doesn't mean that we are seeing things as they are. I don't have to tell you how many men were imprisoned in dungeons for teaching that the world is round, and that's because the world saw it flat, and it was not going to accept anything other than the appearance that it saw through eyes. And I don't have to tell you how a few years ago, we grownups were ridiculing the nonsensical children who were looking at science fiction cartoons about people flying through space and satellites going around in the air. And now the children have a laugh on us because it is being done.

You see, we are not seeing things as they are. We are seeing them as our finite senses present them to us.

Stop condemning. Stop criticizing. Stop judging. "Judge not after appearances. Who made me a judge over you?"[1] Stop all of this. Lift this mesmerism from yourself that finds condemnation in you. Oh, I know you have faults, and so have I. We're not proud of them, and we don't want to perpetuate them, but we're going to if we keep on criticizing and judging and condemning ourselves. If we are going to call ourselves mortal and material, we never will rise out of that phase of existence.

Let us begin our spiritual healing ministry by realizing, first of all, that God is the creative principle of all that is, that God constitutes the substance and essence of this universe. God is the substance of the form of this universe.

If you can do that, you will refrain from accepting or judging by appearances, and you will not be tempted to try to heal somebody or something, but you will stay within yourself and judge righteous judgment, stay within the Garden of Eden, which represents your spiritual domain, the state of divine harmony.

Righteous judgment knows, "In the beginning, God. God created all that was made; God looked at what He had made and found it very good."[2] Are you able to hold to that truth? As ugly appearances stick up their heads, are you able to overcome the temptation to be fooled by them? Non-reaction to appearances is a demonstration of your faith in God's ability to govern His universe.

Abide in the Truth
When Tempted by Appearances

"If ye abide in me... let my words abide in you...." [3]This means if you abide in truth, "if you know the truth, then the truth will make you free."[4] But this knowing of the truth cannot be just at a moment when faced with discord or disaster. It is folly to believe that we can pick a truth out of the air just in a moment of need and then wait for the next disaster to come before reaching for another one. This is making an aspirin tablet out of truth. To abide in the truth means to live in the truth, and you don't live for an hour. Living is a lifetime activity. You live twenty-four hours of every day. Therefore, you must live in the truth; you must abide in the truth and let the truth abide in you twenty-four hours of every day. Dwell in the truth. You can't dwell anyplace for an hour. Dwelling is a lifetime job, just as living is.

Now, the question is, what is truth, and how do we abide in it? And there, of course, you have certain statements or principles which have been revealed as truth, and these are the principles we abide in when faced with any contrary appearance. To understand this, you must understand that we are dealing with a world of lies. For instance, the truth is that God is Spirit, and God is infinite, and God is power. Therefore, God is infinite spiritual power. There can be no other power.

Now this is the truth, but the lie, the appearance, the tempter that we meet every day is that weather is a power, that the stock market index is a power, that the economic level is a power, that infection and contagion are power, that epidemic is a power, that the evil that exists in the minds of men—tyrants, politicians, whatnot—that this is power. This is the temptation; this is the tempter; this is the lie; this is the appearance with which every single one of us is faced, including Jesus Christ in his ministry when he had to face the tempter in the wilderness and had to face the tempter in Gethsemane and had to face the tempter in poverty and disease and the deaths of his followers.

Now, granting that these temptations exist, these appearances, which we call discords, inharmony, evils— to know the truth means that wherever these negative or erroneous appearances touch us, whether we see them, hear them, taste them, touch them, or smell them, our immediate realization is "God is Spirit, God is power. All power is spiritual. There is no physical or mental power." Then, by knowing the truth, you have nullified the appearance, you have nullified the belief in two powers, which is the source of that appearance.

There is only the Garden of Eden which exists, and we're in it as long as we will not be made to accept appearances, judge by appearances—as long as we're willing to judge righteous judgment.

Righteous judgment says, "In the beginning, God; God created all that was made. God looked at what He made and found it very good." That's the truth. Ye shall know that truth.

And then as these ugly appearances stick up their heads, don't be fooled by them. Declare within yourself: "I can't be made to accept good or evil. I accept God, alone, as constituting the Garden of Eden."

Judge Righteous Judgment, Beginning With Yourself

Sooner or later you must be willing to put off this "I" that is full of earthly error, resentments, injustices, inequalities, and declare within yourself, "I am ready to assume my true identity; I am ready to awaken to the light of my being; I am willing to accept the Master's statement that I am to 'call no man on earth my father,'[5] that I am to acknowledge divine sonship for myself." Until you do that for yourself, how can you love your neighbor as yourself? You haven't started to love yourself, and you do not love yourself until you acknowledge your true identity.

You're not supposed to love your human self. It really isn't any good. Even when it's good, it isn't very good. It isn't your human self that you love. You can only love God and His universe, His world, His creation. You can only love God and the offspring of God. You can only love your spiritual identity because it is your perfected Self. Then, unless you're one of the few madmen of the world who catch this vision and then think it refers to them exclusively, then you'll begin to look around at this world, and you'll say, "Aha, I have been judging after appearances. I have been using the scale of good and evil, the very thing that threw us out of the Garden of Eden. I've been clinging to the very barrier to heaven."

Now, judging neither good nor evil, let me judge righteous judgment. Well, what is righteous judgment except for the knowledge of my identity? Nothing else is righteous judgment. It isn't righteous judgment to say, "I'm nearly good," or, "I'm three-quarters good." It isn't righteous judgment to see a person of thirty and say, "How youthful you are," and then look at another one of sixty and say, "How old you're getting." This isn't righteous judgment. Righteous judgment is to be able to look at the young and the old and see Christhood, immortality, eternality, spiritual perfection.

You are not only on earth but of the earth until the moment comes in which you realize that "the Spirit of God dwells in me." You are the "man of earth" until the realization has come to you that as men or women, we are nothing, nothing, less than nothing. And it is only as the Spirit of God touches our consciousness that we are awakened, enlivened. We are the walking dead until the Spirit of God touches us, and we know that through us, this Spirit must be allowed to flow to all mankind.

And the manner of it is to realize that in the face of every appearance, whenever a human appears to us, we are to lift up the Son of God in them and realize God incarnate in them. Whenever an appearance of sin, disease, death, lack, limitation or disaster presents itself to us, we are instantly to

realize that in the presence of God, realized, in the presence
of the realized Christ, temporal power is not power.
Whether that temporal power appears in the form of sin,
disease, death, accident, war, nature, or weather, we realize
that in the presence of the realized Christ, temporal power
is not power. In heaven or on earth, there is no greater power
than *I Am*.

> All appearances are sense-objects—
> not of God, or Truth.
>
> Wisdoms of *The Infinite Way*

Close Your Eyes to the Appearance

If you are going to look at this world with your eyes,
you are never going to be able to believe in God because all
you can see, hear, taste, touch, and smell is finiteness, just
finiteness: limitation, sin, disease, death, stupidity. Once you
close your eyes to the appearance and ask yourself, "What is
the Garden of Eden?" you will hear the "still small voice,"[6]
and even while you are looking directly at sick, sinning, or
dying man, that Voice will say to you:

> *This is my beloved Son, in whom I am well pleased.*[7]
> *Fear not; it is I.*[8]
>
> *I, God, constitute all being in spite of every appearance to
> the contrary. There is only one I; therefore, It is I; be not
> afraid.*

The metaphysical principles of The Infinite Way are
absolutely consistent, and they are based on this: that God
is Consciousness, the infinite Consciousness, and that man
and the universe are this Consciousness formed, expressed,
and since God is incorporeal Spirit, man and the universe
are incorporeal spirituality. Therefore, just as you have never

seen God with your eyes and never will, neither have you ever seen man or this universe with your eyes. You have never yet seen a tree. You have never yet seen a flower as it is in the Garden of Eden, in the consciousness of God. All that you have seen with your eyes is a finite concept of God's creation built on the universal belief in two powers. Therefore, you have seen concepts that are sometimes good, sometimes bad, sometimes young, sometimes old, sometimes sick, sometimes well, sometimes alive, and sometimes dead.

But, remember, these are not creations of God. These are creations of man—manmade concepts—so that when you look over here at me, you don't see me. You see a concept that you have formed in your mind of me. And therefore, if I ask my neighbor to describe me, you wouldn't recognize me, because that is not the "me" that you have formed in your mind. If you could speak to my mother, you'd never recognize me at all because she has a different concept of me. Do you see that? None of you has ever seen me. Now, if you are in meditation sometimes and you reach a high enough consciousness, you may then see me and know me exactly as I am, but that will only be when you have no concepts of me, and you have risen above the mind and behold with the vision that God gives you.

Now then, remember that the basis of our metaphysical work is that God is Consciousness and that this entire universe including man is that Consciousness formed or expressed but in Its image and likeness, of the same substance, same quality, same quantity, same nature, same character, so that all that is true of God is true of man and the universe.

Now, in the human world, where you are ignorant of truth, you are constantly being faced with sin, disease, death, lack and limitation, and evil of all kinds. In ignorance of truth, you accept this world at face appearance, and you pay the penalty for it.

If you have been taught, spiritually taught, you will instantly recognize that this is a mirage, this is appearance, and the Master taught: "Judge not after appearances, judge righteous judgment."[9] Having eyes, do you not see through this appearance? Having ears, do you not hear through this appearance? In other words, you are not to accept appearances of good and evil at face value; you are to accept them as a mirage, an illusion, a form of malpractice, or hypnotism. But above all things, never accept them as something that has to be healed, reformed, changed, or corrected. See through the appearance.

Now, it makes no difference that you are going to meet, every day of your life, with material laws and mental laws and legal laws. Every day of your life, you are going to meet up with appearances of sin, false appetite, disease, evil men in government, and spiritual wickedness in high places.

Every day of the week—you can never avoid it. Don't think that you can go away to a convent, or a monastery, or an ashram, and avoid it. You'll take the world right with you, and the newspapers will shout, and the radios will blare. Never believe that you are going to get to cloud nine where you are not faced with appearances because it will never happen. And as a matter of fact, the higher you go in spiritual realization, the more of it will be brought to your doorstep because the darkness loves to come to the light to be dispelled.

I have been asked many times, "How do you stop thinking?" And I have found one way. The minute I can look at any person or condition and know that it is neither good nor evil, my thought stops, and my mind becomes quiet. That is the end of it because then there are no thoughts left for me to think about it: I do not think good of it, and I do not think evil of it. All I know is that it is, and then I am back at the center of my being where all power is. Our mind is restless only when we are thinking about things or persons, either in terms of good or evil, but the mind is at rest when we surrender all such concepts.

Overcome the World of Appearances

Now again, according to appearances and according to human belief, there are properties there, unlike the nature of good, or God. There's no use of denying that, so far as the human picture is concerned, because there it is. But we are not dealing with appearances because the nature of our treatment is: Judge not after appearances; judge righteous judgment. If you judge after appearances, you will be mixed up in the powers of this world, and you will not "overcome this world." [10]

The kingdom of heaven on earth means the attaining of that spiritual consciousness in which you do not judge by human standards or physical standards. You don't judge health by conditions of the body; you don't judge wealth by the amount of dollars but by the attainment of freedom from concern about the body and the purse. Therein is spiritual freedom. Freedom, spiritual freedom, is freedom from concern about the world.

The achievement of that freedom, the achievement of that spiritual consciousness which results in that freedom, comes to us through the consciousness of those who, in some measure, have attained freedom from concern for this world—what the Master called "overcoming this world." "I have overcome this world."Yet he still ate, he still drank, he still walked the earth, and he still wore clothes, but he says, "I have overcome the world. I have overcome my concern for this world." And what enabled him to do it was the point upon which the unfoldment of The Infinite Way is based.

If we judge life from what we behold with our five physical senses, we are hypnotized to the world of appearances, and we are thereby in bondage to person, place, and thing. As we become unhypnotized or dehypnotized so that we do not look at the world as it appears to be, we find an entirely different situation.

I will use the illustration of the theater. Let us suppose that we are in a theater watching the performance, and we have observed the villain doing his worst, and have developed a concern for what he will do to the hero and the heroine in the next act. However, if we are theater-wise, we will not be concerned about the villain in the piece since we know that there is a greater authority: the author of the play.

The villain, in and of himself, cannot be a villain. The villain, in and of himself, can do nothing to the hero, or the heroine, or the action of the play. The author and the idea of the play in the consciousness of the author determine what the villain will do and what will happen to the hero and the heroine. Always remember that the good characters in the play cannot be good any more than the evil characters can be evil. The determining influence throughout the play is the mind of the author.

Once this is established in our thought, we do not look to the good characters or the bad characters for anything except the excellence of their performance, but the idea of the play is the activity of the mind of the author merely expressed or carried out through the characters on stage.

We might learn to adopt that method of looking at life in general, and instead of fearing what this person or circumstance or situation can do to us, and instead of being overly excited about the good that this one or that one may bring about in our experience, we might look behind the scene to the Infinite Invisible, which is the mind of the author, God.

"God is the author and finisher of our work"[11] and our world. And if we look to God, the one Mind, the infinite Intelligence, and the divine Love of this universe, we will find that regardless of what any individual or group of individuals may appear to be doing, in any given moment, in the final analysis, the decision rests with the great author, God—the one Mind, and the one Soul of the entire universe.

I remember so well a woman coming to my office in California in great tears and self-righteous horror because her husband was an alcoholic. And that would have been all right if it was only his business, but he had gotten to the place where he wouldn't work, and she had to work. And not only did she have to work, but she had to give him her money to buy the alcohol. And that, to her, was going a little bit too far.

But there it was, and there he was at home, and the only day that he got out of bed was on her payday. That is when he went down to the store to buy some whiskey. She was fed up with it, and now, I guess she got spiritual too and wanted to know what I could do about it, spiritually. And as I sat there talking to her, I said,

"You know something; it comes to me that your husband isn't an alcoholic at all; it's you, and you've almost got me being one."

"I don't know what you mean."

"Well," I said, "you seem to be more afraid of alcohol than your husband."

She looked at me and said, "Well, I am. I see what it's doing."

I said, "He doesn't think it's terrible; he likes it. A difference of opinion there." "Yes," I said, "you believe alcohol is bad, don't you?"

"I certainly do."

"And yet the basis of our work is that there's neither good nor evil. What are we going to do with that?" I said, "Let me put it this way. Suppose your husband wanted that money to buy Coca-Cola; would you object?"

"No, I'd gladly go to work, and he could have all the Coca-Cola he wanted."

"Well then, Coca-Cola is good, but alcohol is evil, so there we are back with Adam and Eve."

"Now," I said, "your husband thinks it's good, and you think it's evil. Now you're deadlocked, and I guess that's the way you're going to stay for a while unless you can see what I see: that Coca-Cola isn't good, and whiskey isn't bad; that there's no power in either one if all power is in God."

"Now," I said, "that's the way I see it. God is the infinite all-power, and besides God, there is no power for good or for evil."

"What does that mean? What am I supposed to do?"

"Well, you go right home, and you tell your husband you've made a terrible mistake, that you don't think that whiskey is so terrible after all. He can have all he wants of it."

Huh-uh! Ah, no, that was going too far! But then she went outside, sat in my outer office a little while, came back later, and said,

"Well, I'm not getting anywhere this way. I can't do worse that way, so I'm going to do it, but it's very difficult."

"Try it; see."

So she went home, and she waited for the proper time, and when her husband wanted whiskey, she said,

"Oh yes, sure, here it is."

He looked at her, but he made no comment. A few days later, he came to her and said,

"You know, there's no use drinking this stuff. They're just making wartime whiskey again. It has no power."

And that's how he was ultimately freed. He couldn't drink it anymore. It just didn't give him the kick. And gradually, he saw what he'd been doing.

Now that's an extreme case, but it happened. It bears out the principle that I'm trying to bring to you, which has evolved in The Infinite Way. The principle is that there is neither good nor evil in any creature or form; that all good is in the Invisible. All power rather is in the Invisible acting through the visible.

> When living out from the center of Being, you are
> untouched by the thoughts, opinions, laws, and theories
> of the world. Nothing acts upon you because you do
> not react to the world of appearances.
>
> Wisdoms of *The Infinite Way*

Find God Enthroned

If you are going to hold man in condemnation to his faults, you are going to push him further down into the ground, where he will never have an opportunity to rise into wholeness of spirit and mind and body. So if you hope not only to be healed but to be a part of a spiritual healing ministry, learn first of all never to condemn those whom you would help. Learn never to look within them for the error that's holding them.

Learn never to look to their mind, to their body, or their conduct for anything of a negative nature, for if you find it there, you will only be finding it in your mind, reflected in them. For it isn't there where you're looking. "He isn't in the tomb; he is risen." No one is in the tomb; "he is risen."[12] So don't look for error in your patient or your student; it isn't there.

Look into your patient's, your student's heart and mind, and find God enthroned. And don't stop looking, and don't stop searching, and don't stop declaring it until it comes out in manifestation.

Some of them will give you a hard battle before they yield, but don't you be ensnared by it and come to the conclusion that they're a little too wicked, or a little too materialistic, or a little too unloving. Don't you be ensnared by appearances so that you judge after appearances.

You prove your position in God's ministry by being able to look any and every appearance in the face. Even if you have to keep looking at it for years, keep right on declaring it:

Thou art the Christ of God. Thou art pure spiritual being. Christ sits enthroned in thy being. Thy mind is an

*instrument for God. Your very body is the temple of God.
God is the very soul of you.*

First, you must accept, you must be able to feel in your
heart that what I'm saying is true. Then, you must be willing
to go out and practice it. Sit each day—two periods, three
periods, four periods—in contemplative meditation or
prayer, contemplating God and the things of God, and
see how that operates in your particular experience. Then,
invite God to reveal His light within you, to give you grace,
to open the blind eyes, not the physically blind eyes, the
mentally-dulled or spiritually-darkened eyes, so that "I may
inwardly see Thee, Truth, Life."

Pray that "I may be molded in the image and likeness
of God to be a servant of God, never telling God what I
want, but always reminding myself that God's will be done
in me, not my will be done through God. God's will be
done in me. Mold me in Thy image and likeness. Make me
a fit instrument through which Love can flow. I can never
be that fit instrument while I'm hating, judging, criticizing,
condemning—only while I purge myself, even while I
do laugh at the mistakes of 'man whose breath is in his
nostrils,'[13] but never judge it or criticize it or condemn it in
a censorious manner."

All the Christ-mind is, is the mind of a person who does
not accept or believe in two powers, who does not sit in
judgment or condemnation on any person or thing.

> In the spiritual life, you place no labels on the world.
> You do not judge as to good or evil, sick or well, rich or poor.
> While appearances may show forth harmony or discord, by
> not judging, you merely know Is,
> and let that which truly Is define Itself.
>
> Wisdoms of *The Infinite Way*

The Prayer of Forgiveness and Release

What do I want? "Seek ye first the kingdom of God and his righteousness."[14] Seeking the kingdom of God means seeking the realm, the realization—let's use that word, the "realization" of God. It means pray and meditate and ponder God until that realization comes. And his righteousness differs from yours and mine, from the human standard of righteousness. In his righteousness, you'll find that he condemns no one. He judges, criticizes, and condemns no one—not even the woman taken in adultery; not even the thief on the cross; not even the boy born blind, probably because of syphilis.

Now, he condemns no one, so the righteousness of God—which we must seek and emulate—is a state of consciousness in which we do not judge, criticize, or condemn. That doesn't mean that we approve of evil; it means that we understand that every person on earth is subject to the temptations of their environment, and so forth, and may at any given moment be a devil and in the next moment be a saint. Therefore, we stand by with help but without judgment, criticism, or condemnation or any belief that because they're in sin that they are in some way cut off from God.

So you find that to come to the kingdom of God means to come into a state of consciousness which loses bit by bit, of course, the temptation to judge, criticize, condemn, to hold in evil. You find that God's righteousness is embodied in the word "forgiveness." The nature of God is to forgive. How many times? "Seventy times seven."[15] Infinity. So you say, "Ah, but he sinned against me yesterday, and the day before, and the day before. How much longer must that go on?" I don't know how much seventy times seven is, but at least seventy times seven. That's how long it can go on if it will, and each time there must be forgiveness.

Therefore, if we have not reached that state of consciousness in which we can find it within ourselves to be forgiving, at least in the sense of "Well, Father, if I can do nothing else, I can say, 'Forgive them their sins.'" In other words, come to a state of mind where you wish no punishment on anyone, even for their wrongs. That's quite a place to come to, but we can approach it by degrees, even if we can't attain it in a moment.

Then, seeking the kingdom of God and His righteousness means seeking a state of consciousness in which we approximate that divine state of righteousness, that divine state of consciousness; somewhere in which we are forgiving, in which we are praying for the enemy, praying for those who despitefully use us.

You see, the prayer of forgiveness and the prayer of release is one of the greatest powers that can take place in human thought. There is nothing quite as powerful as the ability, as it's developed, to attain a measure of forgiving-consciousness; of a willingness to see our enemies go unpunished, but that's what we must come to. We must desire punishment for no one; we must desire evil for no one, we must desire only that each be released in the law of God.

> The Lord hath taken away thy judgments, he hath cast out thine enemy: the king of Israel, even the Lord, is in the midst of thee: thou shalt not see evil any more.
>
> Zephaniah 3:15

There must be a conscious release every day. I do not care whether we are talking of Americans or Russians, of the government of the United States or Russia. I do not care whether we are talking of Chinese, Spanish, or whatnot: "Father, forgive them; for they know not what they do."[16] Then you will find the release that you bring about within yourself.

To fit myself for God's government, which means the government of Love, I must make myself an instrument through which Love can flow. And that means I must not permit myself the indulgence of wanting God to destroy my enemies or my nation's enemies. Rather, I want God—if I had the power to want anything—I want God to forgive them. If I had the power to ask anything of God for my enemy, it would be: "Open his eyes that he may see; open his ears that he may hear; fill his heart with the Christ." This attitude on my part is love. It's not personal love; I'm not doing it. I'm opening myself for It to flow through.

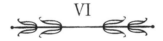

VI

WHEN WE ARE TEMPTED TO ARGUE OR FIGHT: "DON'T FIGHT 5!"

AS LONG AS there are persons fighting evil conditions, there will be evil conditions to fight because the mind that believes in two powers is still creating conditions of good and evil. Only when we withdraw power from them, when we cease fighting them, will these evil powers cease to be.

The moment that you can be tempted to fight a person or a sin or a disease, you are engaged in a battle that, in the end, will destroy you. Why? Because in and of itself, it has no power, but you are giving it the power against yourself.

We may be confronted with evidence of misunderstanding, hate, envy, jealousy, or malice. What difference does it make? It's an appearance. And right where the appearance would seem to be, God is. God is. God is. God is. God is all that we deal with. We do not deal with beliefs, with persons, or with conditions. We deal only with the word "God."

In illustrating this, I have brought to your attention these beliefs which appear to us as appearances, which ordinarily we would seek to overcome through God, through treatment, and prayer. But don't make that mistake. Don't try to overcome material law, mental law, moral law, any law. Always recognize that you are dealing with one law. Anything else may be there as an appearance, just as 2 x 2 is 5 may pop up in your checkbook some month, but that doesn't mean you have to believe it. It isn't true, and you don't have to work against it. You have to merely recognize that 2 x 2 is 4, and the 5 goes of its own accord. Don't fight that 5! Don't try to overcome it. Don't set up mental warfare against it. Just recognize 4, and 5 will disappear of its own accord. As you recognize spiritual law as the only law, all other claims of law disappear.

So it is that we in The Infinite Way have left behind the theological belief that there is a God-power that does things to error or evil, a God-power that fights the devil or fights sin or fights disease, and we have accepted as our principle that Spirit is Omniscience, Omnipotence, Omnipresence, besides which there is nothing else. Therefore, what we have to demonstrate is that in the presence of spiritual power, there are no powers of sin, disease, lack, accidents, unhappiness or any other type of human misery; that these can only exist, these negative things, in the absence of spiritual power, just as darkness can exist in the absence of light. But in the presence of light, there can be no darkness.

There is no argument about that. All spiritual presence and power are termed "light"—"the light of the world,"[1] the light that lights the way, the light that lights your footsteps, your pathway—light, light. All through mystical literature we have the light, and this light never battles darkness, and the light, which is Christ, never fights any form of discord.

Jesus never fought sin; he forgave sin. He never fought disease; he just said, "Open thine eyes,"[2] or "Pick up thy bed and walk."[3] He never fought disease; he never argued with it or against it. There is only one record of his fighting, and that is when he threw the moneychangers out of the temple.

My personal belief is that it was not a historical event. He was merely telling his disciples that we have to throw the moneychangers out of our consciousness; we have to throw these negative qualities and destructive qualities out of our own consciousness. This is the temple. "Ye are the temple of God, even your body is the temple of God,"[4] and it is the negative beliefs, superstitious beliefs, evil beliefs, sensual beliefs, greed beliefs, lust beliefs—these are the moneychangers, the materialistic sense that has to be cast out of our temple, out of our consciousness. Otherwise, the Master taught: "Resist not evil. Put up thy sword; those who live by the sword will die by the sword."[5] I am convinced that the "light of the world" does not argue with darkness or fight darkness or try to remove darkness, but rather the light, being the light, no darkness can exist in its presence.

Now, Scripture tells us that "In thy presence is fullness of life; Where the Spirit of the Lord is, there is liberty."[6] It doesn't say, "Where the Spirit of the Lord is, there is a battle." It doesn't say, "Where the Spirit of the Lord is, there is a fight with error," but on the contrary, "'Where the Spirit of the Lord is, there is peace.' 'Where the Spirit of the Lord is, there is liberty.' 'In thy presence is fullness of joy.'"[7]

It doesn't indicate at all a battling sense, a fighting sense, an overcoming sense. Rather it indicates that where God is realized, there is peace because there is nothing to contend with: light does not contend with darkness. In the presence of light, there is no darkness. In the presence of "the light of the world," there is no sin, no disease, no death, no lack, no limitation, no unhappy human relationships.

So for us now, here is our question: If I accept this as a principle, I must demonstrate spiritual power or spiritual presence, the presence of God, and that's all. I must go no further than this because in the presence of spiritual power, in the presence of spiritual presence, in the presence of spiritual light, there is no darkness.

Until you can reach a state of consciousness that doesn't get frightened at the name of atomic bomb, cancer, consumption, polio, paralysis, blindness, deafness—when you can arrive at that state where those words do not frighten you—and you say, "Oh, that's a lie," then you are in the healing consciousness. But as long as these names or appearances still make you want to do something, you're hypnotized. You're accepting a lie as if it were a fact.

Now, this is the experience of those who have accepted God's government and recognize when temptation is being presented to them. In other words, those on the spiritual path would instantly know when they are tempted with the headlines of an epidemic or a war, or age, or false appetites that abound in the world. They would immediately know that the devil was tempting them, and they would reject it. "Get thee behind me, Satan, for you are no part of my experience. I am God-governed."[8]

To illustrate that, let me bring you back to the experience of the Master when he was tempted by the devil. The devil made certain propositions to him, and to each one of these he said, "Get thee behind me, Satan."

The rest of the world does not even recognize that it's being tempted, and before it can recognize that it is being tempted, it has fallen into the particular cold or grippe or flu or cancer, or whatever the prevailing temptation may be.

For this reason, those who make meditation part of their experience are always prepared to resist the tempter regardless of what form temptation may come. In other words, to awaken in the morning and have a brief period of meditation even without words is acknowledging, "I of my own self can do nothing with this day that lies ahead of me. I am going to admit God, the government of God, into my consciousness."

Whatever the form of temporal power, we are being presented with the principle that we are not seeking a power. We realize the non-power—the non-power of appearances, the non-power of the carnal mind, whether the carnal mind appears as poverty, whether it appears as unemployment, whether it appears as hate, or bigotry, whether it appears as a political or a religious weapon. We need no power to overcome it.

We need to realize its non-power, the non-power of the carnal mind, and then we need one thing more. We need secrecy. These are the principles that must be kept sacred and secret in consciousness so that "the Father that seeth in secret shall reward thee openly."[9]

> Acknowledge God as the substance, law, cause, and activity of all that is, and immediately refrain from meddling physically or mentally in the without. Get back inside yourself, and there resolve all appearances.
>
> Wisdoms of *The Infinite Way*

Rest in His Word

Now, we are facing half a dozen human problems not only in our national life but also in our international life. Any one or two or three of those could tear the foundations out from under our entire civilization. We have the opportunity, if we are willing to tackle the problem, of putting up that sword, of relinquishing our confidence or faith or hope in any human administrations, or human plans, or human agreements, and coming right down to our spiritual basis and asking ourselves: Do I have the courage to take advantage of this opportunity to come out from under the law and live by grace? Do I have the courage to declare within myself, "I must no longer have faith in 'man whose breath is in his nostrils'[10]; I must no longer have faith in princes, or potentates, or powers, and retire within myself for an assurance of an inner grace"?

Now there, in two words, is the secret of our harmony: inner grace. I can't define it for you or analyze it. I can't give you an intellectual discourse on what inner grace is. I can only tell you that it is the answer to every problem, whether it is one of your individual health or one of our nation's or world's collective health, or whether it is one of your individual supply, your family's supply, our nation's supply, or the world's supply. The answer to all of it is an inner grace.

There is no such thing as peace on earth and goodwill to man by any human means ever discovered because peace on earth and goodwill to man has been the aim of the human race since long before 2000 BC. Try to think of how many governments have been formed, and how many different principles to bring this peace on earth and goodwill to men, and no way has yet been discovered, and yet the Master says there is a way: the way of Christ. Christ is the solution. Not the first coming of Christ, not the second coming of Christ, or the third coming of Christ—just the coming of Christ to individual consciousness. But the coming of Christ cannot be described or analyzed or dissected.

There, too, you have to understand that the coming of Christ means an inner grace, and an inner grace means the coming of Christ, and both of these mean nothing more or less than an assurance within that, "He that is within you is greater than he that is in the world."[11] And when that assurance comes you can rest in it, you can relax in it. "In quietness and in confidence,"[12] you become a beholder of this inner grace as it goes out as a presence before you to establish you, to open for you one of those mansions in the Father's house.

Of course, it has always been true: peace and prosperity and health are possible, and they have been demonstrated time and time again but always by the same means—by means of the Christ, by means of enlightenment, by means of spiritual revelation and realization. "To know him aright is life eternal."[13] "To know him aright" is to be so receptive and so responsive that He may reveal Himself within even as a feeling of assurance, as a feeling of an inner peace, always remembering this: You do not need a power, and that is what is disturbing the world today. It is looking for a power. That is all it is trying to do—find a power—and the only powers there are are destructive powers, and there are no good powers. All powers are destructive because all powers can be divided into good and evil. They must all be destructive.

The only thing that is not destructive is "resist not evil."[14] My presence, "My peace I give unto you"[15]—this is not destructive. The Christ—this is not destructive. The Christ raises the dead, heals the sick, feeds the hungry, opens the eyes of the blind, opens the ears of the deaf, but it isn't a power because the Master says, "What did hinder you?"[16] There are no powers.

Start to think for a moment that you who are on the spiritual path are not seeking for a power. You're not looking for a power to overcome the Russians. You're not looking for a power to overcome depressions. You're not looking for a power to overcome diseases, infections, contagions, or epidemics. You are not looking for a power. You are abiding in God. You are resting and relaxing in God. You are not seeking a sword, not a physical sword or a mental sword. You are not seeking powers. You are not seeking plans; you are relaxing and resting in the assurance of an inner grace "that goes before you to prepare places for you, to prepare mansions for you."[17] You are relaxing in the assurance of My peace.

The Christ peace doesn't mean overcoming your enemies except for the enemies that are within yourself, and that is what the Christ does. The Christ empties out "those enemies which are of our own household,"[18] and never believe that your enemies are anywhere else. The enemy is always of your own household, and that means within your own being. And your enemy is always a belief in two powers, a belief in two presences, a belief in two lives, a belief in duality, ignorance—ignorance, that's our enemy.

And the peace that Christ gives is enlightenment. It is not a power over powers. It is enlightenment, the enlightenment that dispels ignorance, the enlightenment that dispels darkness, doubt, and fear. Once you realize, individually, that you are not seeking a power to heal your diseases, not even the power of God; once you realize, individually, within yourself, that you are not seeking a power, not even the power of God to give you supply—all you are seeking is God's grace, all you are seeking is My peace—you will soon find that without the sword, without taking up battles, that you can do as the Hebrews did under Hezekiah: rest in His word.

Not a Teaching, but an Experience

How do we bring the divine Presence into our affairs? Meditation and inner communion—not just knowing the letter of truth and being satisfied. If we maintain our contact, we will live under God's government. It must become an experience. Is the Christ real?

There's never any lack of subjects to treat because there is the threat of world war; there is the threat of economic depression; there is the threat of Asiatic flu; there is the threat of elections. There is enough going on in the family life, community life, national life, so that anyone can sit down a dozen times a day and say, "How can this situation be met?" Well, there's no human thought that will meet it. If truth books would do it, there are enough of those published. If knowing the truth that's in books would do it, there's been enough "truth knowing" going on. So the next step is the transcendental experience itself because this is what The Infinite Way has been saying in every book: This is not a teaching; this is an experience. And whatever teaching there is merely leads up to the experience.

And now we are in that era of The Infinite Way when we must approach every problem from the standpoint, "Now there's no human thought I can think, and there's no truth I can know with the mind that is going to solve this. Therefore, I must be about my Father's business. I must be listening. I must know that *I* in the midst of me is God, and let It utter Itself; let the 'Voice utter Itself that the earth may melt.'"[19] And therefore, I am developing receptivity.

Each one of us who is very actively engaged in healing work is working from that standpoint. We have reached the understanding that my human thought is not God's thought, and God's thought is not my human thought; therefore, my human thought is not power. Even when my human thought is saying a lot of words of truth, it isn't power.

There is a mind that is called "the mind that was in Christ Jesus,"[20] that is, "higher Consciousness." There is a higher Consciousness, and when It is on the scene, the earth of error melts. Therefore, the meditation or prayer or treatment, which is to be effective, is to be one in which that transcendental mind is actually realized, felt. When I can feel It, when I can know, then It is on the field. It is caring for the situation.

It All Has to Do with "Ye"

The change has to come from within. There's no use of changing it on the outside. You have to change it from within. The healing has to come from within, and so the healing in your individual life and mine has to come from within our being, not from without, and the healing in our national life and international life has to come from within and not from without.

Set aside one meditation period each day—and a few minutes each time will be sufficient—to sit in meditation with the inner ear opened. That is all: no praying, no asking, no seeking, especially no desires to be fulfilled. Just meditate with the inner ear open, and then go about your business.

Give a specific period to this each day, and do not let yourself watch for results. In due time, fruitage will appear in some form of harmony within yourself, your home, your family, or your business, art, or profession.

As fruitage appears, raise your consciousness to take in the weather, elections, national, and international relationships. Remember that none of these subjects enters your thought while in meditation. You may not even think of peace on earth. Just be still. Listen with the invisible ear for the inaudible Word. You are thus ushering in the kingdom of God on earth as it is in heaven.

All power is in the hands of the Infinite, the Eternal, and it operates through grace. How do you make this come true? By knowing it. This truth cannot make you free without you knowing it. You have to ponder truth, meditate upon it in your innermost secret sanctuary, and it will establish itself externally in miraculous ways.

Recognize that the truth which is within you is greater than all that is in the outer world, rendering null and void the weapons of this world. This principle will establish individual freedom at every level of human life through an inner communion with the Spirit. These ideas established in consciousness—pondered, meditated upon, communed with inwardly—will establish themselves outwardly.

The Master, in his entire ministry, made it clear that one of the most important words in Scripture is the two-letter word, "ye."

> *Ye shall know the truth, and the truth shall make you free.*[21] *As ye sow, so shall ye reap.*[22] *If you sow to the flesh, you reap corruption. If you sow to the spirit, you reap life everlasting.*[23] *If you dwell in the secret place of the Most High, none of these evils, the snare, the pit, the fall, none of these will come nigh your dwelling place.*[24] *If ye abide in my word and let my word abide in you....*[25]

So you see that whether or not you become free of the discords of this world will have nothing to do with a religion, a religious teaching, or a religious teacher. It all has to do with "ye."

Devotion to the Search,
Invitation to the Feast

When Gautama, the Buddha, first realized that there was sin, disease, poverty, and death, he was so horrified to find that such things existed on the earth that a torment sprang up in him, to such an extent that he was able to leave his princely position, his enormous wealth, and probably what is more important to any man: his wife and child. He left every bit of that and wandered away as a beggar, as a seeker after truth so that he might discover the great secret that would remove these sins, diseases, limitations, and poverty from the earth. It was such a passionate call with him that he followed any teacher and any teaching that promised to lead him to the answer. For twenty-one years he roamed and wandered. For twenty-one years he sat at the feet of one teacher after another, followed the practices of one teaching after another, always with one heart hunger: "What is the power; what is the presence that will remove these evils from off the earth?"

After he had given up all hope that the teachings and the teachers could reveal this to him, he wandered into meditation, seating himself, we are told, under the Bodhi tree. There, he meditated day and night until a revelation was given to him: "Why these things are not real; they are illusions. People merely accept them, then fear them, hate them, love them, worship them, when they have no existence except in the mind of man, the mind that created and continues those conditions."

And you see, it wasn't God that forced Itself; it wasn't truth that forced itself on Gautama and made him the enlightened Buddha. It was Gautama's devotion to the search for God. The very passion he put into it, the very sacrifice of himself, the very willingness to travel all of India wherever there might be a glimpse of truth—he forced the way until rising to sufficient heights, truth was able to reveal itself to him.

In the same way, if you wish to be a master of music, or a master of languages, or a master of literature, or a master of art, God can inspire you, but you must dig, search, study, and practice, until that which you are seeking opens up within your being. I do believe this: that it is God that plants in us the desire to find God, and without God performing that initial function, we never could, and we never would succeed. I believe that. I believe that it wasn't I who had the knowledge or the courage to sit through sixteen years of reading thousands of books, studying, reading, praying, meditating, compelling myself to sleep only three to three-and-a-half hours a night, and spending the rest of the time in prayer, meditation, and healing work. I couldn't sit here and tell you that I can take credit for that, that I could do that. There was a power of God in me, forcing me to do that, but there is no God who could do it for me, no God who could save me those years of sitting alone, working alone, trying to penetrate the veil, get into the mysteries, rise to a higher state of consciousness where I, too, could behold the risen Jesus, the ascended Christ. Only God could make Gautama stay twenty-one years on that path, but only Gautama could persist and fight and pray until the veil parted and the vision became clear. So with us.

Stop believing in some miracle-working power of God that can come down to earth and change you and reveal things to you while you sit there as a spectator in a moving picture theater. It isn't so. The burden is upon you and me to lend ourselves to the search and to remember: There isn't anyone in this room who hasn't received that same spark that Gautama received, or that Jesus must have received, or that Saul of Tarsus must have received to turn him into Saint Paul. The fact that we are here; the fact that we can sit for hours at a time, quietly and at peace with a message of God, with the word of God; the fact that we can spend hours a day in these writings and recordings, that we can devote the amount of dollars that we do, that is the proof that we are not doing it. The Spirit of God has touched us to the search, has invited us to the feast.

Without the Sword of Offense or the Armor of Defense

You are not going to bring God's government on earth. God's government is already here. You are opening your consciousness to the truth that the kingdom of God is established on earth, that God is fulfilling Himself, Itself, on earth as it is in heaven. And the way in which you do that is this. As you become aware of the inharmony and the discord of the earth in the form of sin or disease or tyranny or misgovernment or bad government—as you become aware of discords and inharmony of a physical, mental, moral, or financial nature, remember that you make no effort to correct them or heal them or improve them. To go out into the world with the armor of Oneness means to go out without the sword of offense or the armor of defense.

Liberty is not gained by fighting or by crusading for it, but by keeping it sacred and secret within our consciousness, living it and granting it to others, and thereby watching it spread to the world. Crusades do not change anything because they do not change the consciousness of the individual. Attaining spiritual, economic, or political freedom is not accomplished by the outward attempts people make to gain these ends. Consciousness must be lifted out of its humanhood, out of its belief that self-preservation is the first law of human nature, into the Master's idea of loving another as we love ourselves, and more especially must it accept the revelation that no man on earth is our father. There is one Father and one great brotherhood.

We know that by withdrawing from the use of the world's weapons, we have found the only weapon that will establish peace on earth. We know that when we mentally withdraw from opposition, we know that when we sit inside ourselves looking out upon the world without the use of force, even mental force, we have the secret that heals disease, that reforms sin, overcomes lack and limitation. In the same degree, we are united with every individual on the face of the globe even if most of them have not yet become aware of us; even if they have not yet become aware of the love that we feel for them; even if they have not yet become aware of the fact that we have drawn a circle and included them in it; we know it, and knowing is enough because that knowledge transmits itself to those around us.

Our function in life is not to fight the evils of the world with the weapons of the world. "No weapon that is formed against thee can prosper,"[26] if you do not take up the world's weapons. If you do, you may find yourself defeated. Our way is to take up the spiritual armor, the spiritual sword, the sword of the Spirit, which means prayer and realization.

The Battle Is Not Yours

The world work in which Infinite Way students engage is not fighting evil persons or evil conditions; it is withdrawing power from them, and the students become such clear transparencies that the Christ can flow through their consciousness and dissolve the pictures of sense.

We cannot have any degree of mystical or spiritual consciousness as long as we have good and evil, two powers, personalization of good or evil, or consciously or unconsciously battling evil, trying to overcome it—whether to heal disease or sin or fear or lack. I know that only in proportion as our consciousness accepts the truth that "ye need not fight, the battle is not yours,"[27] are we able to be that consciousness which does not take up the sword—physical battles or mental battles.

So in normal everyday conversation, especially with those who are not on this path, in speaking of the weather, the climate, germs, and all other so-called material powers, we are not going to argue with anyone and try to show how bright we are, or how stupid. "Agree with thine adversary."[28] I do not start an argument with anyone who is talking about what bad weather, bad crops, or bad times we are having. It is not so important what we do in the way of lip service; what counts is what we are doing within.

The promise that is made is this. There is a principle of life which we have not known, which even though stated in Scripture in the first commandment of Moses, repeated as the basic commandment of Christ Jesus, nevertheless, is ignored by the world: God is the only power. Besides God, there is no other power.

Therefore, your attention is drawn to the fact that you can go forth from here and look upon any form of discord as long as you do it silently and secretly and realize within your being, "Thank you, Father. Besides God, there is no other power." As you learn to relax and give up the struggle against error, you will learn the real nature of error, its illusory nature, the fact that error exists as a belief accepted in thought and then fought. It exists as an appearance which we look upon as a reality, an entity. It is almost like looking at the horizon out on the ocean and saying, "I don't think I'll take the Lorelei. It will run into that horizon, and then where will we be?" That belief limited people on earth for thousands of years. In fact, it's only been a matter of six hundred years since people were willing to break through that terrible horizon where all ships would fall overboard into the deep, deep nothingness. Now you see the horizon doesn't exist as an entity; it doesn't exist as a concrete thing. It exists as a false appearance, and the moment an individual knows that and knows that he can't be fooled by the sky sitting on the water because his intelligence tells him that, then he gets into a ship or an airplane, and off he goes with no fear.

In the same way, we witness the car tracks, the train tracks come together in the distance and decide that we won't get on the streetcar or the railroad train because just a short distance ahead we're bound to run off—those tracks coming together that way. Our intelligence tells us that the tracks coming together in the distance are not actually an existence, an entity, an identity, a thing; it is merely an illusory picture that isn't out there at all. It's up here in the mind.

Eventually, you will come to see the same thing regarding evil conditions of mind or body, erroneous conditions of persons or circumstances. You will begin little by little, if you practice, to understand that you must not fight the people and conditions of the world. You must rest and relax, secretly and sacredly declaring within yourself, "Thank you, Father. I accept the first commandment. I accept the fact that besides God, there is no other power."

"Put up thy sword; those that live by the sword will die by the sword," and I ask you to accept that statement with a higher meaning than you have thought of heretofore. "Put up thy sword." Accept that; stop fighting the evil conditions that beset you and begin to face them with the realization that because of omnipotence, these evils have no power. "Put up thy sword." Don't fight the particular evil that's bothering you because the harder you fight it, the more power you give it, and the stronger it enmeshes you. Whereas if you can relax—and you only can if you catch a glimpse of God's omnipotence—if you can relax in the realization,

Well, where I am, God is, so what difference does it make what happens? Where I am, God is. Nothing can happen to me that isn't happening to God, and there isn't any power to make it happen. There is only omnipotence or God's power, and that which is not of God is not power.

Now, these are the things that you take into consideration to spiritualize your consciousness and to attain "that mind that was in Christ Jesus." You must consciously and concretely realize that if there is a law on earth, it is God's law, and it is good. You stop fighting that which the world calls "laws." In the same way, if you acknowledge God as infinite, then if there is any activity in this world at all, it must be the activity of God. You cannot fight what appears to be a discordant activity since you've realized only one activity.

If you fight or look to God to overcome some other activity, you will lose. If you look to God to overcome anything on earth, you will lose.

When you realize that "as in heaven so on earth, God is infinite"[29]; then you know, "the battle is not yours." Only in the attaining of that consciousness can you come into harmony. Otherwise, you will always go around with a chip on your shoulder, fighting persons, sins, diseases, false appetites, lonesomeness, poverty. One condition after another will arise in your experience as long as you are a fighter. Once you realize God as one and can sit back and look out on the sun, the moon, the stars, nature, and tides and realize how wonderfully God operates; see the birds in the air and the fish in the sea, see how wonderfully God operates, then you learn to sit back and say, "Ah, yes. 'God is in His heaven, and all is well on earth.'"[30]

As long as we have not purified ourselves, we cannot be at peace. Let us not forget that we cannot purify ourselves once and stay that way any more than we can take a bath once and stay clean. Purification is a continuous process, not for a year or two, but forever as far as I am concerned. It is "praying without ceasing."[31]

In the beginning, purification of our selfhood does not have anything to do with trying to become better human beings. That is only the effect of the purification. The purification itself means the ability to "have that mind which was in Christ Jesus," meaning the mind that does not judge, criticize, or condemn, that does not accept two powers, and that can impersonalize and nothingize. That is all there is to self-purification, but the act of self-purification by this means results outwardly in a changed state of what appears as human consciousness.

> God is not power. When you reach the center of
> Consciousness, you find a complete stillness—
> a deep well of Silence. It is not power since there is
> nothing for it to be a power to, or over: It just IS.
>
> Wisdoms of *The Infinite Way*

VII

WHEN WE INDULGE
IN CONDEMNATION

WE ARE TOLD, "if so be the Spirit of God dwell in you, then are you sons of God,"[1] and that's what happens. You are no longer finite. You are no longer mortal. You are no longer people who were born and will die. "Now are ye children of God, if so be the Spirit of God dwell in you." How do we know when the Spirit of God dwells in us? When we can meet the world as we met each other here tonight, in a spontaneous feeling of love and joy in meeting each other, in rejoining each other, when we can wake up in the morning and feel that way to the world, then we know that the Spirit of God dwells in us when we no longer condemn the people of this world. I don't mean by that, approve some of the nasty things that people do, but when we stop holding people in condemnation for it and realize, "Father, forgive them. They know not what they do."[2]

When we stop our heckling of people, when we stop our fault-finding, when we acknowledge that the world is returning to us what we are sending out into the world, then is the Spirit of God dwelling in us. When we have learned to forgive the offenses aimed at us personally, racially, religiously, and nationally; when we have learned enough of forgiveness, then the Spirit of God truly dwells in us, and when we are obedient to the ninth commandment, which is "do not bear false witness against your neighbor."[3]

Ordinarily, that is understood to mean that you shouldn't gossip or tell tales or repeat scandal about your neighbor, but in The Infinite Way, it has a far deeper meaning than that, far deeper. To "bear false witness against your neighbor" is to accept them as human beings—even good ones. To say that so and so is good or healthy is to bear false witness against your neighbor because you are holding him in thought as a finite human being, who was born and who will die, who may be good today and bad tomorrow.

To obey this commandment of not bearing false witness against your neighbor, you have to stop believing that your neighbor is good or bad but understand spiritual being. We have to see each other not as good human beings, but as spiritual beings, immortal, eternal, having no good qualities and bad qualities, having only the qualities of God, which are spiritual.

You see, if the qualities of God were good, they could lapse into bad. They would be pairs of opposites, but God has no pairs of opposites. That which is of God is infinity and eternality; therefore, it can't be white or black; it can't be good or bad; it can't be beautiful or unbeautiful. It is a state of invisible, spiritual being, and that's what you are, and that's what I am.

If you could only realize it, this that you see here isn't me. This is my body, so if you are looking at this and judging, you are judging unrighteous judgment because *I*, Joel, am invisible, and you have never seen me, and you can't see me.

There's only one way that you can see me. If you can get still enough and quiet enough so that you come to a state of spiritual realization, then you can see me as *I Am*; that is spiritual and perfect, and that is what happens in healing work.

In that universe of God, there can be no inharmony and no discord. In that perfect universe of God's creativeness and God's maintaining and sustaining nature, where Intelligence and Love are the major factors, no discord or inharmony ever appears. That world is called "Eden." That world is called "the Garden of Eden." That world is called "divine harmony," or it has another name, "spiritual consciousness." Into spiritual consciousness, no error ever intrudes. No form of error ever intrudes into spiritual consciousness. Here you have the basic premise of God's being and God's function in our experience.

There remains only one question to be answered. How then does the serpent come into this Garden of Eden? How does error eventually intrude into this spiritual consciousness and bring about the conditions that we know as sin, disease, death, lack, limitation, wars, depressions, accidents? Well, this you will only learn if you practice the principle of neither good nor evil, practice this principle until you see that the only reason these discords have come in to make up our universe is that back in this so-called Garden of Eden was accepted the belief in good and evil.

Now, you and I are entertaining, in some measure, the belief of good and evil. We all know those things that we call good, those things we call evil; those conditions we call good, those conditions we call evil; those persons we call good, those we call evil. And from my experience, I can say to you that that is what you are going to perpetuate as long as you insist on having this belief of good and evil making up your life. And I say to you from experience, that in proportion as you can overcome the belief in two powers, good and evil, in that proportion will the discords and inharmony be ruled out of your experience and out of the experience of all who come within range of your consciousness.

Practice Seeing God's Creation

You can begin to apply this in a very simple way by going into your home where you may have birds, or pets, or children, and begin right there with "No longer will I think of you as good. No longer will I think of you as evil, but I will look upon you as God's creation, created in His image and likeness, having the qualities of God. 'All that the Father hath is thine,'⁴ and I will henceforth see you only in that way." When you go into shops to market, watch the difference when you learn to look on the clerks as if they were neither good nor evil, and refuse to bestow any praise or condemnation on them, calling them neither good nor evil but children of God, servants of the Most High.

Watch what happens in your immediate family as you begin to unlearn what you know about your husband or your wife or your child or your parents, and begin to go back to their original Selfhood, which was created in the image and likeness of God. Realize that in and of themselves, they have no qualities of good or evil, but all they are is that which God constituted in them and of them and through them. You will quickly perceive that these errors of conduct and thought will lessen as you lift both praise and condemnation.

No man is good, although he may be the instrument through which God's good flows. And no man is evil, although he may be the outlet through which the world's sense of evil may flow. Paul revealed that to us when he said,

"The good I would, I do not; the evil that I would not, that I do. I find in me no sin, but a sense of sin still bothers me."[5] In other words, I am not a sinner, and I have no desire to sin nor any pleasure in it, yet I find myself sometimes being the instrument through which sin takes over. So says Paul, and so say all of us: the evil that we would not, we sometimes still do, even though we know better. And it is not because we are sinners. Left to ourselves, we would never even think a wrong thought, but this universal sense of sin is so great that it sometimes overpowers us.

The overcoming begins when we realize that it is not I who am the sinner, but a sense of sin that would disturb me or take over in me. In the same way, it is not I, who am good, but I who am an instrument through which God's good will flow in proportion as I recognize God to be the source of good, instead of myself.

Begin in small ways to withdraw from the pets and persons about you, the condemnation and praise in which you have held them. Begin to look through to the fact that God alone constitutes their being, and it is God's quality that expresses Itself in them and through them. As you behold in small ways small beginnings, a change taking place in you and those around you, you will know that you have found the principle.

Now, since we are dealing with the carnal mind as a belief in two powers, and as we are meeting this belief so that the effects of the belief in two powers shows forth less and less in our experience and in the experience of those who come to us, it must be clear to you that this is the way of wiping out of human consciousness, all human consciousness, the belief in two powers and its effects.

You can only do this if you have approached a state of consciousness in which there is no condemnation or judgment. If you are still in the state of consciousness that's blaming somebody for their particular evils or accepting the fact that they are as evil as they appear to be, you are not in that state of consciousness that can help to eliminate it, and you have to work more and more with yourself.

You never have your head in the sand and say there is no evil. You never say there are no evil persons or no evil conditions on earth, but you are able to look at them and see their origin in this universal human belief in two powers. In other words, you are able to impersonalize and then finally nothingize. If you personalize error in any form, you are making yourself a victim of it.

How do we love our neighbor as ourselves? "Thou shalt not bear false witness against thy neighbor." "Oh," you say, "I don't. I don't repeat scandal, rumor. I don't malpractice." Well, now let's get together on that. To bear false witness against our neighbor is to believe that our neighbor is human—even a good human. That's malpractice, and it is bearing false witness against our neighbor. Why? Our neighbor is the Son of God.

Purification

You can see that the moment we allow any universal belief of hate, envy, jealousy, or malice, we aim it at ourselves. There is no God punishing us. Do not ever believe there is. We set in motion the law. "Inasmuch as ye have done it unto the least of these my brethren,"[6] ye have set the law in motion that will come back to you. "Inasmuch as ye have not done it unto the least of these my brethren,"[7] ye have set in motion the law that is going to come back to you, you see. It is ye—"as ye sow, so shall ye reap."[8] It is not going to bother your neighbor on either side. It is ye. And it is not going to be visited on your children unto the "third and fourth generation."[9] That is another lot of nonsense. It is going to come back to the individual.

If we think of our neighbor as a human being, we malpractice him, and that belief of human beings will come back and make us a human being again. And a human being means partly good and partly evil, partly healthy and partly sick, part alive and part dead, part rich and part poor. In other words, humanhood is made up of the pairs of opposites. Humanhood is made up of good and evil. And the moment that we start to think of this world and people in it from the standpoint of humanhood, we set in motion the malpractice that comes back to us.

In other words, we must have a period each day of what I call "purification." Throughout the day, I am going to express human thoughts about people in the world. But at least once a day, I must sit down and purify myself by knowing that no matter what human judgment I may pass or what human correction I may give anyone, it is only on the surface and the appearance world.

Actually, I know that thou art spiritual. I know that I am thou and thou art me, and He is us. I know this. I know that there is no evil in anyone. But in the human experience of appearances, there are times when I must correct somebody and sometimes in a way they do not like. There are times when I am bound to have some harsh opinion or judgment of people in high places, but underneath I am saying, "Father, forgive me. I know better." I purify myself constantly because even though I may have to indulge human emotions during the day in some circumstances and with some people, inwardly, I do not mean it. It is very much like chastising a child, or as some parents still do, punishing them. Even when they do it, they do not hate the child; they do not mean what they are doing. It is a surface thing to make them wake up. The few instances where parents let go and get mad at them, sometimes they "kill" their children. But you see, that is because they enter into that punishment, and they do not know their strength or the child's weakness. But ordinarily, when a parent corrects, chastises, or even punishes a child, it is a surface thing.

Even though we may have harsh things to think about some of the people in the world, let us at least not mean it. Let us at least have a period during the day when we agree, "I close my eyes, and I am in complete spiritual consciousness, and you are there—everyone, everyone—because 'God is no respecter of persons,'[10] and we are all here embodied in this divine Consciousness. There is only one great big plate of glass, and it is molded into a thousand different forms. There is one infinite Consciousness appearing as three billion people. Only when the eyes are closed, and I'm looking down here can I realize this is the divine Consciousness of every one of us. Therefore, I am in your consciousness, and you are in mine."

Now, the thing that has to make me careful is that anything I think about you will come back at me. That is where purity is necessary. That is why it is necessary to be pure in our relationships with each other because the moment that we let ourselves get too human, we drag ourselves down into humanhood again. Do you see? What we are thinking of the other, we are doing to ourselves.

Becoming a Center of Love

And so it is that you must take the attitude that Jesus Christ took: "Neither do I condemn thee."[11] In my heart, at this instant, I release every individual from criticism, judgment, and condemnation. I pray that no man be punished for any sin but rather that he be forgiven, that his eyes be opened to the Christ-light. In this moment of spiritual communion, I have no envy in my heart. I have no desires in my heart, no jealousy, no greed, no lust, no animality. I set this world free. There is nothing it has that I want. Since "I and the Father are one,"[12] I receive my good by the grace of God, and whatever good should flow into me and out from me, I freely give to all, to every neighbor, friend, or foe.

Now, if you have purged yourself to that extent and can honestly feel that you have released anyone and everyone, then you are ready for your prayers to reach the center of your being because there is no obstruction. Scripture tells us that "love is the fulfilling of the law,"[13] so do not try to get the law to operate in the absence of love, and love means forgiveness. Love means forbearance. Love means to be inwardly clean: clean of hate, jealousy, envy, malice, greed—all of these negative, minor qualities.

It may not be possible to go through an entire day or night without some of these negative emotions creeping in on us. That is why we became human beings instead of remaining in the Garden of Eden, but we can purge ourselves twice and three times a day, so we look every man and woman in the face and say, "I have released you into the realization of your God-being. I know that you and the Father are one, and 'all that the Father hath is yours.'"

If you only knew what it meant to come into the presence of a person who is not sitting with a mind full of criticism, judgment, or condemnation, or, more positively, to come into the consciousness of a person who understands and forgives and forgets; come into the consciousness of a person whose gentleness is such that no thought even enters their secret mind of any harsh nature. Thus do you see we become a center, and everyone who comes within range of our consciousness feels what the world calls "love" because forgiveness is an attribute of love. Understanding is an attribute of love; understanding the universal nature of these evils is love. To understand them is to forgive them. To forgive them is to "love thy neighbor as thyself."[14]

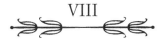

VIII

WHEN WE SPREAD FEAR, RUMOR, HYSTERIA, AND MASS CONFUSION

O N EVERY HAND mankind is gripped by fear in the face of nerve-shattering world conditions, and those of us who have been able, even in a measure, to see the unreal nature of the evil rampant in the world have not only the responsibility of releasing people from their fears but, in releasing them from their fears, preventing the greater tragedy that their fears may bring upon them. People do not fear because they are cowards; they fear because they are gripped by universal hypnotism that makes them act in ways foreign to their nature. It is mass hysteria, having its foundation in ignorance.

The evils that befall us are not in God or man but rather in the conditioning that we have received through the ignorance that has been foisted upon us from time immemorial. In other words, every time that we give power to a person, a thing, or a condition, our consciousness is showing forth its conditioning, and to that extent, we become victims of it. It might come as a surprise to see how easy it would be for some person, either for a specific purpose or an experiment, to show us how quickly we could be made to distrust one another, and then, in the end, fear one another. It has been done over and over and over again.

It is a very simple thing to condition the minds of persons who are not alert so that they unthinkingly accept the opinions, thoughts, and beliefs of others and respond robot-like to individual suggestions or mass hysteria. If we listened to all the propaganda and the opinions of others, very soon we would be fighting not only with our families but with our neighbors and the whole world. The question is this: To whom do we give allegiance? To whom do we surrender our minds and our thoughts? It is very difficult for persons who have not been taught the value of meditation to turn within to the Presence for Its guidance, instruction, and wisdom. Instead, they rely on opinions gathered from newspapers, magazines, and television broadcasts and thereby fear every headline as if it could be a threat to the life, which is God.

Do not come down to the world's level of gossip and rumor, hearsay and fear, and worry. You are not going to be saved by the Republican Party or the Democratic Party. You are not going to be saved by communism or capitalism. You are not going to be saved by a change of administration. You, who have taken the name of Christ, are going to be saved by the degree of your realization of Christ. I can guarantee you liberty, freedom, health, wholeness, harmony, wealth in Christ, through Christ, regardless of what evils come nigh the dwelling place of those still dealing in and with material sense. You are not going to put your faith in human documents or weapons of warfare. You are going to rely on your realization of Christ, the divinity of your being, and you are going to let it show forth the harmonies of God in your experience. And thus, you will be that "man who has his being in Christ."[1]

Contribute to the Peace of the World

As in the days of Christ Jesus, today, the world is faced with a choice: on one side are all the temporal power and material force of Caesar; on the other is the "still small voice" calling "Come unto me, and be saved"[2]; on one side "the sword" and on the other "the armor of Spirit." "Choose you"[3] resounds through every land. Will you trust material power or spiritual Presence? Shall we meet Goliath with a battering ram or a pebble? It is a time for decision: "Choose you." On one side is the mass hysteria of fear; on the other, the inner stillness and peace in the assurance that "I will never leave thee…. [4] I am with you always even unto the end of the world."[5] Goliath challenges. Is there a David?

As long as an individual turns to God for the overcoming of material or mental problems, he will fail. As long as an individual has hope in God to destroy the sins of the flesh or the diseases of the body, he will fail. As long as an individual hopes that God will bring peace on earth and goodwill to men, he will fail. I would not know how many centuries people have gone to church to pray to God for peace. I only know that in my short lifespan we had World War I, II and the beginning of III, and countless days were spent in churches, not only by individuals but by whole nations praying to God to bring peace on earth and God's been a little bit slow about it.

God is very slow about it because God has no power to bring peace on earth. That is something that can be done only by the individuals on earth. God cannot come into this room to establish peace among us. We can establish peace among ourselves. We do not have to war with each other. We do not have to sue each other. We do not have to have any form of argument or disagreement. Oh yes, we can have natural disagreements as to whether you like orchids better than roses. I was not thinking of that. We can disagree as to whether we like berry pie better than lemon pie. I was not thinking of that. I am thinking of the fact that in this human world, we disagree in forceful ways, disagree on subjects of economy, politics, religion, race, creed, and at times are even willing to murder in the name of Christ. Oh yes, "If you don't join my religion, let us arm our brother and go out and slay you, one way or another."

Now, there's no use praying to God about that. God has been prayed to for so many centuries, or what the world calls "God" has been prayed to, with no answer. There is more strife on earth than ever before because there are more people on earth and more races, more nations, more religions, more creeds. But we can overcome war and disagreement, and it is to that end that we are here studying, bringing to light the spiritual laws that will make peace on earth possible for us, first as individuals, and then for the world at large.

We know this: that it devolves upon those who have received spiritual light to be transparencies through which that light reaches the world. As it comes to your attention that there is some form of so-called evil taking place or about to take place—evil of health, evil of weather, evil of human relationships—please remember that it is a call to you, as an illumined soul, to "leave your nets"[6] immediately and retire into a meditation until that particular situation has been met.

Every time you consciously remember that the only life there is on earth is the life of God, you help to allay fear. You help to restore "the peace that passeth understanding."[7] Do not think for a moment that there is going to be national or international peace until peace has been established in our innermost being. In other words, the reason we here are at peace with each other is that we have found a peace within, in each other's companionship. We have found that peace within, and therefore we cannot battle without. And please remember, only when peace has been established in the minds and hearts of mankind will peace be restored nationally and internationally.

Your Consciousness
Operates as Leaven

The person imbued with Christ-consciousness does not go up and down the world battling, but lets his light shine so that anyone who perceives this light in him can go to him and ask, "Give me some of this." The Bible is a revelation of the Christ, a revelation of the infinite nature of God, individually demonstrated, but requiring the activity of truth in individual consciousness to bring it forth. It is the realization that God is not sitting up in the sky and man waiting down here on earth for God to bring peace on earth. Peace on earth comes as an activity of truth and love in consciousness, but it has to begin in the consciousness of an individual, spread from that individual to a group, spread from that group to a community, and so on around the world.

> Another parable spake he unto them; The kingdom of heaven is like unto leaven, which a woman took, and hid in three measures of meal, till the whole was leavened.

Matthew 13: 33

When the grace of God is received in your consciousness and mine, it is not a static and limited "something" embodied somewhere within our frame; it is a light that permeates us and flows out through us and from us. And inasmuch as there are no barriers to the activity of Spirit, this light which we have received as the result of our union with our Source flows out through the walls and windows of our homes into the world and becomes a leaven wherever an individual is raising his thought to God, regardless of what concept of God he may entertain.

In every instance where spiritual light has come to an individual, he has been called upon for that light. Those who have the most, of them the most is expected. Those who have the most of spiritual light are going to be called upon more and more for that light. In other words, it would have been impossible for Moses to have received his illumination on the mountain and then gone away to live the rest of his life by himself enjoying it. It would have been impossible for Elijah and Elisha, for Isaiah or Jesus, or John or Paul to have received their spiritual light and then hidden it under a bushel basket or gone away to a cave somewhere or a mountain retreat and lived this spiritual life unto themselves.

You may say, "Oh yes, that is true in the case of these greater lights." It is equally true, at least proportionately true, of those of us who are lesser lights. In other words, every grain, every speck of spiritual light that we attain, is meant not for ourselves but that it may be used for the benefit of human consciousness until human consciousness is entirely dissolved and nothing remains but that "mind which was also in Christ Jesus."[8]

Every bit of light that an individual receives dissolves some measure of human consciousness or mortal consciousness or carnal consciousness. You may think that the light an individual receives dissolves some of the grosser consciousness of his or her being, but that is not true. That is not true, because no one has any mortal consciousness. All of the mortal consciousness there is is the universal sense of separation from God, universal hypnotism, universal mortal mind, if you will use that phrase.

Therefore, every bit of light that any individual receives is nullifying some measure of the carnal mind, some measure of the vast human illusion. With every grain of light that is attained by any individual, it immediately goes into the greater work of dissolving human sense, material sense.

There is a responsibility on our shoulders to study, to meditate, to do all that is necessary to bring greater light to our consciousness. And now you can see the main reason for it. The main reason is not really you. The main reason is that this light, which touches your consciousness, may flow forth to the world and benefit the world. In other words, that you may become a center from which goes the light of healing, of regeneration, of forgiving, of blessing, of peace, of comfort.

As a student of The Infinite Way, you cannot possibly fulfill yourself until what you are taking in is released. It would be like accumulating money and then locking it in a vault. As a citizen, you would be worth nothing, because it is how you express and release what comes in that determines the quality of your citizenship.

Stop now and think of what this means. The attained measure of spiritual consciousness of a dozen to a hundred students becomes the higher consciousness of an entire community and, in some measure, transforms the lives of all within that larger circle. Does this not make clear why "ten righteous men"[9] can save a city and why a few spiritually-evolved persons can rule out of their communities the grosser elements of human nature and restore a greater measure of the Father's consciousness on earth as it is in heaven? Do you begin to see how it is that eventually the Garden of Eden will be lived again on earth as consciousness is evolved to a divine state here and there around the world by individuals and small groups who thus become the higher consciousness of these communities?

Just think what one little handful of people living in God's grace can do to a whole community. They can change the whole election; they can sway the course of events. Not only that, they can change the actions of their leaders because all leaders—political, religious, educational—are influenced by the mind behind them, the mind of the public. You will find they usually move to carry out what we want and, of course, what we want, most of us, is that they carry out that which will show forth harmony and peace on earth. But there is no way to get it on earth except to have it first in our consciousness. Just as in this room, whatever takes place between us—take my word for it—whether it is love, understanding, cooperation, joy, even healing, can only take place if it is in our consciousness.

We sit inside ourselves looking out upon the world without the use of force of any kind, even mental force, withdrawing all opposition, and this renunciation of the use of the world's weapons is the only means by which peace on earth will be established. It may take years; it may take centuries before "He come whose right it is,"[10] that is, before this is demonstrated on earth as it is in heaven because there are only a few people out of the billions on earth who are consciously practicing the Presence. That little leaven, however, must leaven the whole lump.

Do you not see that if what you are reading is true and you feel it, you will be inspired to live this truth? Then can you see that wherever you are in time or space, if you so love God that you will spend many periods a day, even brief ones, tabernacling in the temple of your inner being with this Presence, one here and one there will be drawn to you? As an individual, you may believe that you can do nothing; you are only one in four billion. But if you look at the great spiritual lights of the past, you will understand how untrue that is, because you will see how one individual called Gautama, the Buddha; one individual called Jesus, the Christ; one individual like St. Paul influenced not only his generation but the generations that followed him and will influence generations yet to come.

Once we have acquired the realization of a spiritual truth, it is ours throughout all eternity, but it is also one that will remain behind in the consciousness of mankind to multiply itself; this is spiritual law.

You May Not Pass By – It Is Given to You

You can see, therefore, that whether you are practicing spiritual truth in your family circle or on a wider scale that you will not make too much of a success if you haven't gotten into the habit of starting your day immersed in spiritual truth. Then, "if you live and move and have your being in God-consciousness, none of these things will come nigh thy dwelling place." "If you abide in the secret place of the Most High,"—if you establish yourself in the realization of one power—"none of these things will come nigh thy dwelling place."[11]

Now, the completion of your protective work is done when you take the next step and realize that the power of good, the power of Spirit, operates from within your being. It does not act upon you. It works out from you and acts upon this world.

In other words, you are the transparency through which the law and life of God function, and they function within you and out from you. Just as the woman who touched the Master's robe was healed because he was a transparency through which this presence and power of good was flowing, so does your consciousness become the transparency or the instrument through which the law of God flows out into this world.

At this stage of your Infinite Way development, unfoldment, or state of consciousness, you are responsible for every picture that presents itself to your sight or hearing. You may not pass by on the road. It is given to men, the human world, to ignore the troubles of their fellow travelers, especially if they are of a different land or different religion or different race or different color. It is not so given unto you. The grace which you have received from God was given to you, not for you; it was given to you as the fruitage of God, which the world is to eat.

"Take, eat of my body, drink of my blood."[12] Give up your grapes to the world; you are a wonderful vine on whom more grapes will grow. And you are spiritually fed and spiritually clothed and spiritually housed, and you know it. Therefore, let your grapes go out into the market, into the world.

At this state of your unfoldment, you owe a debt to God and the world, and that is that you do not "pass by on the other side"[13] of the road, but that you take note of every discord, every inharmony, and bring to bear the activity of the Christ. Be a transparency through which the Christ may dissolve the appearance.

You do nothing, and you do not necessarily have to think anything, but you must be still. You must be still for an instant and let His spirit flow through you to the appearance and dissolve it. You may not pass by on the other side. You are at a state of spiritual unfoldment where you have already been told to "leave your nets"—not to go anywhere or to do anything, but not be concerned about your nets in the face of appearances. Rather, cease your fishing for a moment and be fishers of men. And how? Just by recognition. It only takes a moment, the blink of an eyelash, of an eyelid, the blink of an eyelid, that you may realize that in the presence of Christ, temporal power is not power; "they have only the arm of flesh."[14]

We widen our circle and let our vision go beyond our immediate environment and look out at mankind with the same feeling that we have for one another. That same motive toward the world will bring the world into the circle of Christhood.

Remember that God does not act without a consciousness through which to act. Remember that God must have saints, saviors, seers. Let us put it this way: God must have simple carpenters; God must have princes; God must have simple housewives of whom God makes saints and saviors and seers to send out into the world to carry the light.

Almost all who have attained any degree of spiritual stature in the world have been as simple nobodies as we have been and are. Only the inspired light made them seem to be more than that to the world. In and of themselves, they were nothing; in and of ourselves, we are nothing.

But in our conscious union with God, all that God is I am. "All that the Father hath is mine.[15] The place whereon I stand becomes holy ground"[16] because "I and the Father"[17] are here.

We do not have to do or think anything to release the kingdom of God into the world: we have to know that It is, and be still. It will do Its own work. It may be that the faithful practice of the principles of spiritual living by "ten righteous" men here, and another ten there, will release this power of God on earth. Nobody will be able to take credit for it. God's power has always been available. That is the glory! And no one can brag or boast that he is able to use it. On the contrary, the greater the power that flows from a person, the less the person is as a person, and the greater he is as a child of God. Within ourselves, however, we will know that releasing God into the world brings spiritual freedom and spiritual fulfillment to those who are receptive.

It is this activity of truth that you and I are holding, in our consciousness, and working with, in our consciousness, that not only produces miracles for us but for our neighbors, our families, our communities, and ultimately, for the world at large. Of course, it all has to begin on an individual level. Do not talk these things over with anyone. First, demonstrate them. Let the fruitage come forth in your own experience so that somebody near you will say, "I want some of that. Where do you buy it? Does it come by the pound or quart?"

A Healing Consciousness Releases Others from Fear

Anyone who realizes that the nature of the errors of our lives has been brought about by our ignorance, by our superstitions, by our fears—anyone who realizes this can easily develop a forgiving consciousness. I must say to you from my experience that this is the deepest and finest healing consciousness that can evolve.

It is one thing to heal through knowing specific truths, and this does quite a bit of healing work. But I can tell you that nothing is quite as effective in the healing ministry as a nature that understands the universal fears, superstitions, and ignorance and can thereby say, "Neither do I condemn thee,"[18] and yet never say it openly or outwardly. Always live in that atmosphere of releasing everyone from their hidden fears, hidden sins, hidden omissions, and commissions.

Who would ever voice fear or preach fear who had the inner awareness of an immanent God, of a God "closer than breathing, nearer than hands and feet"?[19] Who would ever "fear what mortal man can do to me,"[20] or what mortal power can do to me, once they attained the realization of an actual God?

The healing ministry, the Christ ministry, which is really for the nations of the world, becomes part of our responsibility, and if there are "ten righteous men" in the city, the city will be saved. How much more so if we develop ten thousand of us in the world who will devote five or ten minutes every day, unselfishly, to a realization of Christ-activity in the world at large, to know that the government is not on the shoulders of premiers and presidents and dictators but that the government is on the shoulders of Christ, and Christ enforces its mandate through these human leaders? Why should we not take at least five or ten minutes every day to realize Christ-government on the face of the earth? I think you will find not only that we will benefit the world, but eventually, we will be that behind-the-scene spiritual group changing things in the human scene, and at the same time, we will benefit ourselves.

To maintain an Infinite Way consciousness, a Christ-consciousness among Infinite Way students, I have asked everyone to agree that five or ten minutes of your day or night belongs to the world in unselfish, impersonal, impartial realization of the Christ, and not only for the allies, remember, but for the enemies as well. As a matter of fact, I would spend much more time praying for the enemies than for our own. That comes nearer Jesus' concept of prayer. He told us so definitely, so distinctly, that "praying for friends and relatives benefits us nothing, profits us nothing[21]; we must pray for our enemies, for those that despitefully use us, for those that persecute us,"[22] and that's about the place for us to begin our prayer.

We are of the few who know what is going to save the world. We are among the few, the few groups in all the world, and we know now what the principle is that is destined to save the world. It is, above all things, the acknowledgment that "no man on earth is our father."[23] There is one universal Father within us, and united with It, we unite with every spiritual child of God throughout the world. Therefore, our love for God constitutes our love for the people of the world. We no longer hate; we no longer fear. We have learned that as long as there are two powers fighting each other, one or the other will win, but it will only be a temporary victory. We know that the principle that will save the world is withdrawing from the use of power, withdrawing into ourselves and contemplating our oneness with God and each other; our ability to forgive; our ability to love; our ability to serve; our ability to surrender the desire for

vengeance, for revenge; our ability to withdraw punishment
from the sinner. We need not fear that that will free them,
for sin punishes itself. But we need not punish; we need not
seek vengeance or revenge. Our function is love, the love
that comes through the realization that our union with God
is our only integrity.

Integrity is the backbone of all relationships. And these
days, what a crying need there is for integrity and ethical
conduct at all levels of human experience! Integrity is
a spiritual quality and stems from God, just as do love
and gratitude. As we maintain our oneness with God by
turning within continually during the day, the integrity of
our actions is assured, and with integrity as the basis, our
everyday relationships are strengthened and harmonized.
We experience the beauty and joy of oneness with each
other as a result of our realized oneness with God. As
with understanding and peace in a family or community,
so integrity among nations, in government, business, and
family relationships, always begins with the individual.
How much integrity are you showing forth?

IX

WHEN WE PERSONALIZE
GOOD AND EVIL

SPIRITUAL CONSCIOUSNESS IS your consciousness when you have no evil to combat, when your evil has been impersonalized and nothingized. That is Christ-consciousness. It is not some other consciousness that is going to come to you. It is your present consciousness when your consciousness is divested of personalizing good and evil or empowering evil. Your consciousness, this very consciousness which is you, is Christ-consciousness in proportion as you are impersonalizing and nothingizing.

Therefore, there is no new consciousness to gain; there is no other consciousness to go out after. It is a purification of the consciousness which we now have, and which in its purified state is Christ-consciousness. In other words, Moses, after his illumination, was still Moses, but with purified consciousness. Jesus was still Jesus but with purified or Christ-consciousness. That is why he was called Jesus, "the Christ," Jesus, "the Enlightened." He was still Jesus, the same Jesus, but now, "the Enlightened." And enlightenment means only one thing: the recognition of these principles. That is what constitutes enlightenment and opens the way for illumination.

The inner experiences that we have, the inner experiences that come to us and the instruction that comes, and the wisdom, the guidance, and the direction come only at those times when we are living in that consciousness of no condemnation, of impersonalization, and they cannot come to us at any other time. That is the full meaning of that statement: "When you go to the altar and pray, and there remember that anyone has ought against thee, first get up and make thy peace."[1]

We have this principle of impersonalizing evil, and this means denying the evil a person in whom, on whom, or through whom to operate. In other words, look upon every evil as if it were being offered by a tempter, as if you were seeing Satan stand before the Master, and you having the ability to say, "Get thee behind me. I am having none of it."[2]

Is it any different out in the world than it is with us in our homes? One of the difficult lessons on the spiritual path is to be able to look without resentment right at those who would rob, deprive, or persecute us, and pray, "Father, forgive them."[3] Until we are able to look through the appearance and know its impersonal nature and non-power, we are not prepared for a spiritual ministry, and prayers from such a consciousness are wasted.

Those of you who have had experience in even a small degree of healing work, among your friends, or your family— if you have worked with the principles of the Infinite Way, you have already proven that impersonalizing evil is about three-quarters of all that is necessary for the healing. In other words, the moment you stop accusing somebody of wrong thinking, the moment you stop blaming someone for being sinful or sensual or jealous or envious or malicious, the moment you stop pinpointing the evil in or as a person, and you begin to see that which is called a mental cause is as impersonal as the spiritual cause—once you begin to perceive that, you are on your way to doing healing work.

If the Kingdom of God Is Within Me, Why Am I Disturbed?

Whenever a threat comes from a government, the head of a government, the representative of a government—whenever a threat comes from any direction, let us remember: "Thou couldest have no power except it were given thee of God,"[4] for God is omnipotent, all power.

Do not forget this: Before there was a Khrushchev, there was a Stalin, and before Stalin, there was a Hitler, and before Hitler, there was somebody else. In the history of the world, there has been somebody all the way back to pharaohs on whom we could pin the immediate problems of the world. But we have gotten rid of pharaohs; we have gotten rid of Caesar; we have gotten rid of the unholy popes; we have gotten rid of a lot of the bad kings and queens of old, and emperors; we have gotten rid of Hitler and Stalin, and still the world goes on building new ones. Why? Because the ax has never been laid at the root of the tree; because we have been lopping off branches and leaving the tree, leaving the life of the tree. And what is the life of the tree that is harassing us? The belief that evil has power. Lay the ax at the root: "Thou couldest have no power over me unless it was given thee of God."

Instead of trying to think up something to destroy the Hitlers or the Khrushchevs or anybody else whose name disturbs you, instead of trying to find a way to overcome them, retire within yourself and ask yourself, "Why was the kingdom of God established in me, and what is its function? Why am I neglecting it? Why am I overlooking it? Why am I ignoring it? Have I never heard that the kingdom of God is within me? Have I never wondered why it is within me, how it got there, what its purpose is, what its function is, and how to bring it forth into expression?"

Well, I will answer the last question first. The way to bring it forth into expression is to look your enemy right in the eye, whether your enemy is a physical, mental, moral, or financial condition, or whether it is a tyrant out in the world or some of the mothers-in-law that we read about. But let us have that same vision,

> *Thank you, Father. Nothing can come nigh my dwelling place; nothing shall enter my consciousness that defileth or maketh a lie because I acknowledge the omnipotence of God. Omnipotence means all-power. The all-power of God means the non-power of the physical, mental, moral, or financial condition.*

We have the opportunity to bring about a purification of our consciousness, which is the preparation for spiritual anointing. First, we must recognize that spiritual anointing can come only to the consciousness that is prepared for it. This preparation consists of the degree of spiritual vision which we attain. The practice of it is in the degree that we live with one power, the degree that we impersonalize both good and evil, and nothingize them. Every step of our journey on this path is one of purification. Sometimes we have to get very hard knocks before we accept purification, and there is a natural reason for this for which no one should be condemned but which should be understood.

Healing is not removing disease from the human being; it is revealing his Christhood, and that can come about only through the destruction of the carnal mind. The destruction of the carnal mind comes only through the understanding of one power, impersonalization, and nothingization. The practice of these principles brings the purification that is the preparation for the anointing.

Now, the man that you see, hear, taste, touch, or smell is not spiritual, good, immortal, or eternal. Close your eyes to the man you can see, hear, taste, touch, and smell. Get inside and declare,

> *Ah, but God is the essence of the real man. God is the essence of this man, woman, or child—not what I see, hear, taste, touch, and smell. That is the man who has to die daily until there is no more left of him.*

But when I close my eyes now, I always begin with the word "God." Never begin with the word "you." Do not pull that "You are Spirit; you are spiritual; you are God. You are perfect." Do not do that in The Infinite Way. Start with the word "God."

> *God is perfect; God is Spirit; God is Life; God is the soul of individual being. God is manifest as individual being. God is incarnated as individual being. God is all-true Being. God is the only law. God is the only law to any situation. Matter is not a law. Disease is not a law. Human belief is not a law.*

Look Above Forms and See God Everywhere

You understand the whole works once you understand the impersonal nature of *I*, once you stop pinning spirituality on a man and saying, "Oh, thou art good" or "Thou art spiritual" or "Thou art perfect." How nonsensical can you get? *I* am Spirit; *I* am perfect; "I and my Father are one."[5] *I* am in "the secret place of the Most High."[6] Ah, that is an impersonal revelation because it permits you to state that. It doesn't pin it onto any individual. It proclaims it as a universal truth.

Never personalize, never restrict or limit God to a specific person or channel. It is like limiting the sun to a specific garden. Look above your garden. See the warmth and light of the sun. The sun is impartial, universal, and impersonal. Look above forms and see it omnipresent as all form.

If you would bring the grace of God into your experience, you must consciously open your consciousness to this truth that "I and my Father are one." The statement alone can do more harm than good because it can give you a blind faith in a statement of truth, and that will not help you. When you declare that "I and the Father are one," you must have some concrete idea in your mind what that means. You must either visualize this tree of life and the branches and realize that you are one of those branches, and therefore it is true that "I and my Father are one," or you must see the ocean and the wave and realize, "If I am a wave, at least I am really the ocean," because there is no place where an ocean ends and a wave begins. The wave is the ocean itself in a form.

Somehow or other you must have the ability to understand how it is that "I and my Father are one." Use the illustration of the tree of life, as Jesus did in the 15th chapter of John, or "As the wave is one with the ocean, so I am one with God," or any other way in which you can make it clear. I have used the example in some of our classwork of glass and a tumbler. Glass is the substance. Tumbler is the form. But how can you separate glass and tumbler? You cannot. They are inseparable because there is no tumbler. Tumbler is only a name given to glass in a certain form.

The Infinite Way reveals that God appears on earth as man. God is the substance and essence, and man is the form. But really, there is no man. Man is only the form as which God-life is appearing on earth, God-mind is appearing on earth, God-soul is appearing on earth.

Yielding Self-Interest

Living mentally means determining what you want and how you are going to get it. Spiritual living is yielding to the reign of God, the kingdom of God. It is yielding desires. It is yielding the self to a receptivity of spiritual guidance. It is not an outlining and a determining of what we want or how we are to attain it. It is yielding—a complete yielding of one's self so that one may be the instrument through which a divine intelligence can operate.

We must reach the place where we can dedicate ourselves to something higher than our interests. We must rise above self to the place where we consecrate some portion of our time to the cause of establishing God's kingdom on earth, holding to the vision that has already entered human consciousness, remembering silently and sacredly that all freedom is a quality and activity of God as much on earth as in heaven, and then let this divine principle open up human consciousness, first in one place and then in another. When an idea's "time has come,"[7] it always finds a way to establish itself on earth.

I think right now of an experience that we had this past year. You will notice all through the writings, a quotation: "He performeth that which is appointed for me to do."[8] I did not know the meaning of it until this past year. I have been using it for thirty years—it shows how we can be blind to our concepts. I thought it meant that God did that which I'm supposed to do. But during this past year, I learned that is not true. He performs that which He gives me to do. He performs His work in me or through me. He does not perform my work. He does not perform anything that is my will or my way or my desire. He performs that which He appoints for me, and therefore, unless I am abiding in "Nevertheless, not my will, but thine be done,"[9] unless I keep myself clear of wanting to do something or accomplish something or be something, I have no access to God's grace. God's grace functions to perform God's will, not my will or not my desire, not my hope and not my ambition. Therefore, I am only under God's grace when I let God perform Its work through me—not help me with my work, but perform Its work through me.

You would be surprised what a difference it makes in your life, once you realize that there is no God around to help you. God is only around to perfect His work through you. He is not around to perfect your work or my work. His function is to perform His work or Its work, and therefore, only when we are in attunement. How do we know when we are in attunement? When there is no "I" around, no personal sense of "I" that wants something, desires something, hopes for something. When we can become a complete blank for the Spirit to work through us to Its will, that is when we know that we are in attunement, in at-one-ment. But as long as there is an "I," Joel around, there is not spiritual attunement.

That is why I repeat the story of having had five practitioners work for me in my last year of the business world and then ended up with no money. It was not because they were not good practitioners; they were. It was that I wanted them to get God to do my will and give me good business, and God does not know anything about my business. God only knows about God's will. And the moment that I was still enough to listen to God's will, I was back on the beam again with an income, only now not through business, but through the practice. It should not be necessary for us to get it the hard way, but it was for me because I was still in that stage where I thought there was a God to do my will. I only had to turn to God, and God would prosper me. Why me? It's a mystery now how anyone could think that there is a God to prosper you or me and not the rest of the world, but there is no such thing.

God is here to prosper the will of God and the way of God and the function of God, and our function is to be the servant of God, the instrument, the transparency as which God can work.

> Go to God as an empty vessel, desiring
> fulfillment in God's way and measure.
>
> Wisdoms of *The Infinite Way*

The most difficult part of our entrance into the spiritual life comes because of this idea of God as a power that is used to destroy other powers, evil powers. We cannot easily outgrow the belief that we can use God. Now, of course, you can understand how utterly impossible it would be to use God. That certainly would take God out of infinity and make it a tool of ours and yet, you would be surprised how stubbornly the human mind clings to the idea of using God, more especially of using God for some purpose of our own.

Let us make it easier for ourselves by realizing that God uses us. We are the instruments of God—God is not the instrument of man. God is not a tool used by man; God is not a servant sent out to do man's will; God is not a servant sent out to fulfill man's desires. God is the supreme will, and we come into that grace when we submit our will to the Divine.

God is love, and we benefit by God's love when we submit ourselves to God's law, God's will, God's love. God is infinite. This makes it impossible for man to use the power of God. Man submits himself to the power of God; man yields himself to the power of God, and then God's grace takes man and lives his life and fulfills Paul saying, "I live yet not I, Christ liveth my life."[10] Not, "I live Christ's life"— "Christ lives my life." God dwelleth in me not as a servant, but as a master. The Master revealed why it is impossible for a man to be a master: "For there is but one master, the Father within me, and I am a servant of the Most High."

In proportion as we give up the idea of using God, as we give up the idea of being the master of God, as we give up the idea of having God do our will, in that proportion are we sowing to the Spirit. In that proportion are we permitting God's government to be "on earth as it is in heaven,"[11] God's government on earth—not man's government— God's government on earth. That is when we yield ourselves to God's government.

God's grace is universal, and to love your neighbor as yourself means that when you do have this God-contact, you pray that it touches all mankind. Then you are surrendering all personal self-interest. You are praying aright. The spiritual path is a way of sacrifice; it is a giving up, a surrender.

There is a greater need for what we have today than has ever existed before, and certainly, in solving the world's problems, we solve our problems because if the world has no problems, neither would we have. If we sat down with one statement of truth and applied it to some national or international problem—well, this one comes to me now: the coming election. Let us forget for a minute that we are American citizens and that we have some personal stake in how the election comes out. Let us say that we are a citizen of some country or other, any country on the face of the earth. So as Americans or Englishmen or Frenchmen or South Americans, we should feel an interest that the United States of America has, at this particular time, at its head, not only a president but a Congress of the highest intelligence and the highest integrity. All right, if we can agree on that, we can, until Election Day, forget our partisanship and our personal beliefs, and we can sit down and say, "All right, if prayer is a power, I want to pray that the United States of America be given the most intelligent and the most honest government possible. How am I to pray?"

Each one might have a different answer, but in one such situation, this is the answer that came to me. My mind went back to when Judas Iscariot betrayed the Master, committed suicide, and there were eleven disciples left. There had to be twelve for them to function properly, so they met to elect the twelfth. Out of all the other followers of the Master, they were to select one. And do you remember what their prayer was? "Father show us whom thou hast chosen."[12] And they all agreed on the one who was to supplant Judas Iscariot.

If we prayed like that, "Father, show us whom thou has chosen to be president, senator, governor," it would be a very

different election than if you and I were to say, "No, my
grandmother was a Republican and my grandfather was
a Republican, and I'm a Republican, too." And somebody
else might say, "Well, I am from the South, and they are
Democrats, and I would not betray my ancestry."

> Any response on a lower plane than pure consciousness is
> from one's self rather than one's Self.
>
> Wisdoms of *The Infinite Way*

Members of One Household

Since God does not function on a personal basis, God
will not do anything for you personally. There must be
within you the remembrance that this that you seek, you
seek for all mankind, for everyone, friend or enemy. It would
be as impossible to channel God into your affairs as it would
be to channel the rain into your garden. If you want to pray
for rain, you had better pray for rain and not specify yours
or anyone else's garden. You will have to be willing for it
to fall on the gardens of all those you do not like as well as
those you do.

When you realize the divine Presence, you must include
the prayer, "Let Thy grace be upon all mankind. Let all men
be receptive to Thy presence." Whether or not they are is not
the point. The point is that you are surrendering personal
interest in the act of loving your neighbor as yourself.

As I permit myself to be God-governed, my life is
God-governed. But I cannot say, "Oh yes, God, I'm ready
for you to govern me." That is not giving oneself to God's
government. To give oneself to God's government means to
accept the laws of God. We have to accept the laws of God,

and we have to act on them. And that means that I must always consciously remember that love is the secret of the religious life; that unless I love my neighbor as myself, unless I forgive, unless I do it unto the least of these my brethren, I am not accepting God's government. I ask for God's government while I continue to live in man's government of "self-preservation is the first law of nature."[13]

Look out upon this world and declare unto it: "Call no man on earth your father.[14] My Father is your Father. Your Father is my Father."[15] There is only one spiritual, creative Principle, and It has created us as members of one household. We are one in spiritual sonship. See what this does to you in the elimination of bias, bigotry, and hate because there is no other way in which we can lose bias, bigotry, or hate. It is not possible to say, "Oh, I am tolerant," for this is a lie. No one is tolerant until they have come to an actual realization of the fatherhood of God and the brotherhood of man. Yes, they might be tolerant in the sense of tolerating somebody, but that is not the tolerance needed on earth for unitedness. We need the understanding of the one Father and the household, the brotherhood of man. Now we are fulfilling the greatest law of the Bible in what we are doing in this minute. We love our neighbor as ourselves.

There is no other way to love your neighbor as yourself except to accept him into your family. Accept him into your heart. Accept him into your prayers. Think of the different relationship that exists on earth the moment you have united with your fellow men under the fatherhood of God.

Try to vision this larger canvas of life so that you do not measure your spiritual life by what it is doing to you and yours and for you and yours alone. Rather, see how the measure of spiritual freedom that you attain is the measure of spiritual freedom that you are giving back to the world, hastening the day of freedom for all.

Now Spirit Functions Your Life

As guests of life, we are only temporary visitors to earth. It is not given to us to possess anything here permanently because we can take nothing with us when we leave except the spiritual treasures we have laid up. But remember that every spiritual treasure that we carry into the next plane of existence is a spiritual treasure that we will also leave behind. It is not finite: it is Omnipresence Itself.

Is there anything or anybody that will be with you to the end of the world except *I*? And could you reach any place before or after *I*? No, always "I and my Father are one." "The place whereon thou standest is holy ground"[16] because *I* am there within you. Be still and know *I* within you is there, is God, and will ever be. "I will never leave thee nor forsake thee;[17] fear not, it is I."[18] Fear not, it is *I. I* the All-presence, the All-knowing, the All-power, the All-loving.

Then let us go about our business each day and let the Father within do the works. For this *I* that is within each one of us is "the Father that doeth the works."[19] Then we are cleansed; we are purified; we are a vessel that is empty. We have no words, no thoughts, and for a moment—it can be a second, it can be a minute, it can be five minutes—we are receptive. We wait. And whether or not we know it, something takes place.

There can be no such thing as a vacuum without it immediately being filled, and this vacuum that we have created by emptying our finite selves is instantaneously filled with the divine Presence which *I Am*. There are times when we consciously know it and feel it; there are other times when we do not. It is of no importance whether we know it or whether we feel it. It has happened! There can be no such emptying out process without a filling up process for these are one.

"Where the Spirit of the Lord is, there is liberty,"[20] and the moment you have emptied yourself of self, made room for the Spirit, the Spirit is there. You may hear those words, "Where the Spirit of the Lord is," there is fulfillment. In the presence of God is fulfillment. Where I am, Thou art, and this is fulfillment.

"The Spirit of God is upon me, and I am ordained to heal the sick."[21] These words are spoken continuously from generation to generation, just as if they were a perpetual tape going out over the air. But they can only be heard in the silence by those receptive. "The Spirit of the Lord God is upon me." Paul reveals that as creatures, you "are not under the law of God neither indeed can be, but when the Spirit of God dwells in you, then do you become the child of God."[22]

When does the Spirit of God begin to dwell in you? It has been dwelling within you from everlasting to everlasting, but from the moment of your acknowledgment of It, from the moment of your realization of It, It consciously functions your life. From the moment of your emptiness, and then your realization, "Fill me. Let Thy mind be my mind. Let Thy life be my life. Let Thy spirit be my spirit." Then it takes place, and it is so.

Then you come to the form of life again, expressed by Paul: "I live, yet not I; Christ, the Spirit of God that dwells in me, It lives my life." It is my bread and meat. It is the resurrection unto my body. This Christ, which I have now consciously permitted to enter and express Itself, this now is the substance of my life, the substance of my body, the law of my life. "I live, yet not I. The Spirit of God that dwells in me, It lives my life." It is my flesh, as well as my bread. It is my resurrection. It restores the lost years of the locust.

Let me be empty. Let the Lord enter consciously, always with the realization that if there be any faults in me, any "hidden faults"[23] in me, that I am purified, that I am willing to surrender, and then watch the miracle in transformed lives because you are not a human being who knows some truths; now you are emptied of being a human being, and you have become divine, by virtue of the Spirit of God which dwelleth in you.

Consciousness lives Itself; you do not live It.

Wisdoms of *The Infinite Way*

X

WHEN WE PRAY AMISS

W E COULD AVOID all the inharmony and discords
of human experience if we knew how to pray, if we
knew the function and method of prayer because prayer
is our contact with the infinite Source that maintains the
harmony, the peace, the wholeness, and the completeness
of mankind. We cannot, by might or by power, make our
life beautiful, but we can fulfill our nature through an
understanding of the function of prayer and its practice.
God created you and me spiritually, in His image and
likeness, imbued us with His life, His nature, His character,
His qualities, and His quantities, and because of that, this
great capacity for fulfillment exists within every single one
of us.

The purpose of life on earth is to bring forth that capacity,
to bring forth that beauty, harmony, and grace in lives of joy
and fulfillment. That is the original purpose of the life of
spiritual man as it was meant to be lived in the Garden
of Eden, that is, in divine harmony. We lost this capacity
because we lost the ability to turn within, to open out a way
to let beauty, harmony, and grace be expressed. We began to
search in the outer realm for the Holy Grail. We traveled
all the way around the world, and for what? Contentment,
peace, joy, harmony, rest! Were we successful in our search?

Of course not, because we had to take ourselves around the world as we traveled, and the self that we took around the world is the self that had not found its home in God. But when the self finds its home in God, it can travel or remain at home and find eternal bliss and eternal opportunities for service, for dedication to God and man, in an exchange of good.

Remember that it was only when Adam and Eve left the Garden of Eden that they had to labor and toil, not when they were under God's grace.

Many people have wondered why for centuries so much praying has taken place, so many millions of prayers in so many millions of churches, and so few answers. In my mail, I read every day the tragedy of people who pray for themselves and pray for their families, and then someone goes out and gets killed in an automobile accident, or somebody comes down with this disease or that disease, and they say, "What is wrong with my prayer?" or "I have tried to live a good life, a Christian life, a life of benevolence, for years and years and years. I pray, and tragedy strikes my home just as much as the homes of those who do not pray." What is wrong with our prayers?

The answer is this: Prayers, regardless of how one prays, never reach God unless, before the prayer, contact is made with God. We are in the same relationship to God as an electrical appliance: it may be a beautiful appliance, complete and perfect, but until the connection is made with the electric current, it cannot operate. And you can pray from now until the next century, and it still would not operate unless actual contact was made with the electric current.

As human beings, we are branches of a tree that are cut off, and our prayers are worthless. Regardless of how sincere, regardless of how deep, regardless of how philanthropical they may be, they are worthless unless first, we have made contact with our Source, unless we have first made contact with God.

If you "abide in the vine," and "if you let these words abide in you, you will bear fruit richly"; but if you do not abide in the vine, if you do not make contact with the Source, "you will be as a branch of a tree that is cut off and withereth,"[1] and praying will not help.

It is for this reason that we meditate, not only before our classes and after our classes and sometimes in between, but we meditate morning, noon, and night, and then in the middle of the night. And the further our students go in their spiritual advancement, the more they meditate until eventually, it is a normal thing to meditate twenty or thirty times a day, counting a day as a twenty-four hour period. Why? Because of the mesmerism of this world—the radio, the newspaper, the television, the neighbors, the relatives— all of these pull us right out of our contact with God. They do not mean to—ah, no, no. "The road to hell is paved with good intentions."[2] I know their intentions are good, but they are disastrous because dwelling on the problems of the world and fearing them will not bring about answered prayer. Being anxious about the conditions of "this world" will not bring about answered prayer.

Answered prayer has its basis in the Master's revelation that we are "to take no thought for what we shall eat, nor what we shall drink, or wherewithal we shall be clothed.

We are to take no thought for our life."[3] We are to seek the realm of God. We are to seek the realization of God. We are to seek the kingdom of God, the realm of God, oneness with God, contact with God, whatever it is that establishes oneness with our Source.

The meditation helps to establish that contact if the meditation is practiced intelligently. Meditation is exactly like prayer in that it must never contain a desire; it must never seek anything of God; it must carry no wish to God, not even the wish that my life might be saved, or my child's life be saved, or my country's life be saved because this is such an utter waste of time that it does not even pay to take time to talk about it.

You only have to review the history of the world since you were on earth to know that every parent has prayed to save its child, and every child has prayed to save its parents, and every man and woman in every country has been praying to save their particular country and their particular flag. What has happened to these prayers?

You see this covers a tremendous subject that you must see: God is not here to fulfill your desires or mine. God is not here to be your servant or mine. God does not exist to please you or me. God, under no circumstances, does anything for you or me, and there is no way of compelling God to do for you or me or mine or yours.

The only correct approach to prayer and meditation is: "Not my will be done, but Thine."[4] Not do for me what I wish done, but prepare me to fulfill Thy will. Let Thy Spirit be in me that I may be a child of God, that I may be one with my Father, that I may dwell in the Father's house, and the Father dwell in me.

God is not our servant, but it is fit that we be servants of God. God is not the son of man; it would be well if the son of man could be the Son of God. In every case, in our prayer and our meditation, we must yield ourselves, our will, our desire to God, and let God fulfill His will, His grace in us.

> Never seek anything or any condition in prayer.
> Let harmony define and reveal itself.
> Let your prayer be letting the IS appear.
>
> Wisdoms of *The Infinite Way*

Praying With the Ears, Not With the Tongue

You have a God of omniscience, all-wisdom, all-intelligence, so that when you pray to God, you can say, "God, cut my tongue out if I try to talk to you. Let my prayers be with the ears, not with the tongue. Let my prayers be listening, not speaking."

Can you accept a God who is divine love? It is asking a great deal. Very few seem capable of accepting a God of divine love because a God of divine love is forever bestowing, never withholding, ever caring. To accept a God of divine love means that we would cut the tongue out before we would ask God for anything because we know we would be dishonoring God with the inference: first, that God does not know our need; and secondly, that He is not loving enough to bestow it. Therefore, prayer must be with the ear, not with the tongue.

Prayer must be with the ear and not with the mouth, and not with the thoughts, and not with the mind. The mind of man will never reach God in prayer. Unless the mind is

still so that it can be receptive to the "still small voice…"
"Speak, Lord; for thy servant heareth"[5]; not thy servant is
telling thee, not thy servant is asking thee. "Speak, Lord;
thy servant heareth," and let prayer be a listening attitude, a
receptive state of consciousness, and with it the desire that
what we hear shall transform us and renew us, not that what
we hear shall bring baker's bread or butcher's meat. That
which we hear shall transform and renew, that every word
we hear shall purify us and make us fit receptacles.

You see, prayer and meditation have to do with this
spiritual realm, the kingdom of God, which is within you,
and harmony, spiritual harmony, wholeness, perfection in
your experience, in your human experience, must come
forth from the kingdom of God within you, or from what
the Master called "the Father within me,"[6] or what Paul
called "the indwelling Christ, the Christ within, the Christ
in me."[7]

Now this, you must remember, is not lip service. It is not
vain repetition. It is not a form of mental exercise. It is an
experience that must take place deep down within yourself,
that area of your being, which is Consciousness or Reality,
and when you have that deep inner experience, you have
touched God, or you have been touched by God. Then it is
that the Son of God takes command of your life and brings
forth harmony, wholeness, completeness, and perfection.

God's power flows through you and me in proportion to
our creating a vacuum, a silence through which it can flow.
Therefore, you can see the importance of arranging your life
so that time is allowed for these periods of silence. Let your
first period be when you wake up at the beginning of your
day. Before you get out of bed in the morning, spend at

least five minutes in reaching the center of your being, in feeling at peace with your inner self. In this way, you begin the day by establishing yourself in the Spirit even before you leave the warmth of your bed in the morning. Wait there in quietness and peace for the Spirit of God as It enters not only your soul but also your body. Feel It right down to your fingertips. Feel It in your toes. Feel the Spirit moving in every part of your body.

Selfless Prayer Is a Gift to the World

Once I realize that when I close my eyes, I am in the divine Consciousness, and I am to bring forth infinity, I must take the next step and realize I am not bringing it forth for myself. There is no plan in the divine kingdom that any one of us has a monopoly on good. Therefore, Thomas Edison could not bring forth electric lights for his home alone, and Henry Ford could not bring forth automobiles for his family. When something comes through, it is universal, and you must be prepared to let it flow. There must be no thought of, "God sent this to me." No, I brought it forth from God, but now it must flow—always, it must flow. There must be twelve basketsful to share, of whatever it is. It makes no difference. If you are not pouring it out like the fruit on the tree, you know what happens: it will dry up, and it will prevent the next crop from coming out.

Ah! You see, this is a theme of prayer. The greatest barrier to prayer is to go within and want something for "me" because there is not any God in there that knows "me." God is there fulfilling Himself, expressing Himself. Heaven forbid that it should ever be for me because He would be cutting off the whole world, wouldn't He?

No, no. When I go within, it should not be for me. It should be for the revelation and the unfoldment of whatever God has. And then, whether it is for you or me, let it come forth, and if it is for you, let us share it. Do you see that? Because the lesser is included in the greater. As long as I go within for the unfoldment of good without thinking of it as "my good," I will have lots of good unfold that I can share, but because of the other, my own is included in it. In other words, I am not left out. But I am left out if I go within for "me" or if I go within for "mine."

If I was to go in and want the health of my child, if there were such a thing as a personal God, can't you hear Him laugh and say, "Why? Is your child better than your neighbor's? What is there that I have that is for your child any more than for your neighbor's child?" So I cannot go in and ask for something for my child. I can only ask for a revelation of whatever children need. Then I have it for my child, but I also have it for all the other children who may come into my experience.

You see how we have been conditioned on prayer? We have thought of going within to prayer to pray for something for me, and we have wondered many times why it didn't happen. What we want to go in meditation or treatment for is universal good: "Father, reveal Thyself. Father, reveal Thy truth." Not the truth about me. There is no more truth about me than there is about you; otherwise, God would be a "respecter of persons."[8] Whatever truth comes through about anyone must be the truth about everyone; whatever truth comes about everyone must be the truth about every individual one.

Therefore, when we pray, don't pray amiss. Just remember, you have closed your eyes; you have shut the outside world of appearances out, and now you find yourself in the divine consciousness of Being, in the infinite consciousness of Being. Now, don't go in there to bring forth a few coppers. Let a whole diamond mine come out. And if it is too much for you, then share it. That's all. But don't limit what is going to come out. Don't go in seeking something for some tiny little purpose or some tiny little person. Let God reveal Himself in His fullness, and then you will find that your needs are taken care of, and you've got these twelve basketsful left to share with others.

The spiritual students of the world have within their power the ability to change the world in this century into a heaven on earth. How? By prayer and meditation, by letting loose this "bread" that they have stored up within them.

To pray spiritually really means to have a feeling that our arms are outstretched, even when they are not physically outstretched, and that we have all the world in our arms and are saying, "Father, forgive them their sins. Father, open their eyes and their ears. Father, I pray that Thy love may shine upon them, that Thy grace may feed and sustain them." This is prayer—when the arms are outstretched, and the whole world is inside: the world of friends, relatives, and enemies. All the world is inside, and we say, "God's love is upon us; God's grace is within us; God's benevolence shines in our hearts." This altitude of prayer brings forth a spiritual response within us and the accompanying spiritual fruitage.

We who have witnessed the power of prayer in our individual experience and have begun to share it with our relatives, neighbors, and community know the richness that enters life through what we pour out from within us. The great masses of mankind know absolutely nothing about the peace that can be found through prayer. They know nothing of a spiritual union among people that makes them love one another regardless of differences of race or religion or barriers created by borders. They know nothing of the fatherhood of God and the brotherhood of man, which unite us in one household of one family. Their lives are drab, and they do not even suggest that there is any other kind of life. Their attention is focused on the thunder and lightning of the world, on the noises of the world, its troubles, excitements, and pleasures. If the masses could know something about the world of the Spirit, some of them at least would begin to open their eyes and desire what we who have learned about a life of prayer have discovered.

Prayer, to be answered prayer, must come from a heart that is purged of personal and selfish motives, a heart that has for its desire that all men may know God's grace. This prayer, silently spoken or thought, not only sets the one who prays free, but it sets mankind free. We can watch it in operation at the level of the family. We can use this silent, secret prayer in our household, confining ourselves to our immediate circle, and pray that God's grace be established. We embrace everyone in our consciousness until we have made peace with them and have attained an absolute conviction that we desire the grace of God to be their experience.

When we begin to see the fruitage in that small circle, then we are ready to lift our vision and go out into the community, to the seat of our government, to cross borders and look each nation in the face, each religion, and make peace.

Go thy way in peace. May God's grace be visited upon you. May you forever know the joy of living in His forgiveness and His love, peace, and prosperity.

Prayer for God's Government on Earth

World prayer work is the most difficult of all because we must, first of all, surrender all concepts as to the solution we are seeking, never praying for a certain event or experience. And the reason this is difficult is that each one of us has decided whether it would be good to have a Republican administration or a Democratic administration and, in some cases, even a Socialistic or Communistic administration. And when we pray, we are praying for this, and there can be no success in such world work. Success comes only with the surrender of material or human desires, and the desire for God's government on earth: spiritual government, not just a different form of human government.

God is Spirit, and the only prayer of a righteous man is a prayer for spiritual realization, spiritual harmony, spiritual government, and spiritual grace.

You need no words, and you need no thoughts; you need the silence of receptivity, the listening ear, and then, whatever truth has to be voiced, God voices. There must be a listening consciousness. Be still. Be still! Don't think thoughts. "Be still and know that I am God.[9] I in the midst of you,[10] closer to you than breathing"[11]—*I* am God. Be still; "in quietness and confidence,"[12] be still. Stop taking thought because by taking thought you cannot change anything in the world. You will only make it worse than it is. Do not take thought. Be still; listen for that voice. Say to the Father, "Speak, Lord. Thy servant heareth," and "when he uttereth his voice, the earth melteth."[13] And it is this that keeps us from becoming egotists and believing that we humanly have power, whereas we are but the instruments or transparency through which and as which the power can act in proportion to our stillness and our quietness.

Never forget that the Master says, "If I speak of myself, I bear witness to a lie; it is not I that do the work but the Father within."[14] And this will ever keep you humble enough to know, even if you stop a storm or a war, it will make you humble enough to know that you did not stop it; you were the transparency through which the activity of God reached human consciousness.

We may pray the highest kind of spiritual prayer, but if in our heart there is not the desire to see harmony, peace, and spirituality realized, our prayer is worthless. On the other hand, we could pray the most orthodox prayer that has ever been prayed; we could pray even as the pagans did. If in our heart there is a desire for peace—I do not mean victory; I do not mean a desire to get your way or my way, your country's way or my country's way—I mean that if there is a sincere desire to see the reign of the Christ on earth, the form of our prayer would make no difference because there is no God listening to the human voice. There is no God listening to Catholic prayers, Protestant prayers, or Jewish prayers. The God that answers prayer is Spirit, and It answers prayer according to the spirit of those who are praying. In what spirit are we praying?

When we pray, we pray universally. We pray that all men's eyes be opened, that the kingdom of God be realized on earth as it is in heaven, that those who are in sin be lifted up and be forgiven, not punished. We never pray for anyone's punishment. Our prayer is that everyone be forgiven. We pray that those who are offending this world, who are against liberty, justice, and equality, be forgiven, that their eyes be opened, and then we will be contributing to the peace of the world.

When it comes to the subject of prayer, the Master has given us the greatest teaching on the face of the earth. "For what you shall eat, what you shall drink, or wherewithal you shall be clothed," and I suppose he meant to go on and say, "about any danger or any destructive element on the face of the globe: take no thought, for your heavenly Father knoweth that you have need of these things, and it is his good pleasure to give you the kingdom."

So you see, this automatically eliminates all forms of prayer in which we turn to God for anything, in which we ask God for anything, in which we expect anything from God because we are able to rest in those words of the Master: "My heavenly Father knoweth my need, and it is his good pleasure to give me the kingdom." And this absolves me from all responsibility for taking anxious thought, doubtful thought, or concerned thought. It relieves me of the responsibility of praying to God for these things because I have the divine assurance that my "heavenly Father knoweth that I have need of these things, and it is his good pleasure to give me the kingdom."

Then what is it that acts as a barrier preventing this good, this protection, this harmony reaching me from God? And in my experience in this work, I have proven that in proportion as I have accepted God as omnipotence and thereby robbed everything else of power, whether it was germs, infection, contagion, paralysis, drought, or tornadoes, in proportion as I have accepted within myself that these are but the "arm of flesh,"[15] temporal power, no power, I have seen it made evident that God is omnipotence and that these things are not power.

Every time you hear a news broadcast or see a newspaper headline heralding some unfortuitous circumstance, you automatically turn away from it in the recognition that this, which you are hearing or reading, can exist only as a picture in the human mind and not as any part of God's kingdom. In God's kingdom, harmony reigns. In such instant recognition, when you have learned to reinterpret the pictures of sense that touch your consciousness, you are praying without ceasing, and yet you are doing it without consciously declaring the truth; this was the high state of consciousness of the Master. He was living in such an exalted state of spiritual consciousness that when a woman pressed through the throng, she was healed by touching the hem of Jesus' robe, without his knowing that she was there. Without any conscious thought on his part, in that exalted state, she was healed. Remember, however, that it was the days and nights that Jesus spent in the wilderness, his years of training and self-discipline, that lifted him into this high consciousness in which he did not recognize any error to be denied or treated. So it will be with you. When you reach the point where you are never aware of any form of error to treat or to deny, your treatments and your prayers will be wordless, yet you will be treating and praying all the time.

Men, judging by human standards, complain
that prayer is not answered. To benefit by prayer,
it is necessary to give up all personal concepts of good.
Do not try to fit answered prayer
into the mold of human desire.

Wisdoms of *The Infinite Way*

PART 4

RETURN TO THE
GARDEN OF EDEN

XI

WHEN PEACE DESCENDS

THE WORLD THAT GOD made in six days is the world that we are making with our labors. We are creating our new world every day with our mental and spiritual labors. We are creating a whole new world for ourselves, a whole new consciousness, and one day we will realize that we have reached it. Our labors have not been in vain. The Christ is risen; we have entered. "My people must enter a period of rest, a Sabbath,"[1] in which life is by grace, "not by might, nor by power, but by my Spirit."[2] And never forget this: It is a real experience, living by the power of God. It is not a biblical phrase. It is a real experience, living by the Spirit of God, living by grace, living in the Sabbath, where you no longer "take thought for your life, what you shall eat or what you shall drink or wherewithal ye shall be clothed,"[3] but My spirit goeth before you.

The movement, the transition from law to grace, is done by you, within your consciousness, at a specific moment. It could be a moment like this one, in which you decide that the time has come to stop living by chance, by averages, by insurance statistics. In other words, the time has come to stop being a statistic, and to move out from among them. Come out and be separate and live under grace. It can only happen in one way. "If so be the Spirit of God be in you, then are you the children of God."[4] Until that time, you are a mortal; you are a human being; you are subject to age, change, limitation, war, peace, depression, boom, health, sickness, life and death, chance, luck, and horoscopes. But when you make the transition filled with the Spirit of God, "then are you children of God, and if children, heirs, and if heirs, joint-heirs with Christ in God to all of the spiritual kingdom."[5]

"Think not that I am come to send peace on earth: I came not to send peace, but a sword."[6] What a strange statement this is to come from a consciousness such as that of the Master! Somehow or other, we visualize Jesus, the Christ, as sitting on cloud nine all the time, in peace, harmony, joy, and completeness, with no rainy days in between. Yet he says, "I came not to send peace, but a sword." A person may interpret this in any way he wishes, but I speak to you about it from the standpoint of what I have witnessed in my thirty-odd years in this work and from my observation. The reason the Christ seems to bring a sword is that our purpose in life and the Christ's purpose in life are two entirely different things.

We think in terms of economic or physical good; we think of peace, security, health, abundance, and happiness, but entirely in human terms, always involving the acquisition of some material form of good to bring us that peace, harmony, wholeness, and completeness. Even nationally and internationally, we depend on a bomb for peace, a frightening concept of the condition required for peace, nevertheless, a fact in this age. In the past, we have depended on armaments to establish and maintain peace for our nation, and individually, we have depended on sums of money or a measure of physical well-being. In our lifetime, however, we have witnessed the failure of all of these to give us peace, security, or happiness.

If you are looking for the peace of the world, do not go to the Christ for it, because the peace that *I*, the Christ, gives you is a peace that the world cannot give. The world might flood you with money, honors, or fame, but it will leave you hollow inside, unsatisfied, and incomplete. But when you feel My peace, you will feel it abundantly, permanently, joyously, a peace that passes human understanding. Then you will understand why "My grace is sufficient for thee."[7] There is no lack where God's grace is. "My peace I give unto you"[8] is spoken from within you to you, from the center of your being out to the circumference.

> *My wholeness I give unto thee; My immortality I give unto thee; My infinity I give unto thee. Never do I withhold; all this is thine.*

Nothing can establish permanent peace in the heart of an individual except for the entrance into the heart of the Christ, the Spirit of God. As peace is established in the heart of the individual, ultimately, it will be established in the world: a peace that comes, not by the knowledge of man, nor by the wisdom or power of man, but by the Spirit of God functioning as the consciousness of man.

Do you know what happens when you discover that Christ is within your being? You are made free! Nobody can control you; nobody can influence you; nobody can take advantage of you; nobody can tell you that you have to burn lights or that you have to burn candles, or that you have to put coins in a poor box. Nobody can tell you what you must do because you have realized your oneness with God, and you don't have to do anything for anybody once you have attained the realization of the Christ within you. You are free. Nobody can tell you your salvation depends on how many prayers you utter; nobody can tell you your salvation depends on how many communions you have, or don't have.

Do you not see that when mankind learns of his freedom in Christ, he is free? After that, no one can hold him in bondage. And that is why each one must learn for himself that he embodies his freedom within himself. His freedom is not dependent on others any more than health is or wealth is. Every good in our experience is dependent on the recognition of the Christ that is within us. Everything necessary to our unfoldment, to our progress, to our need in life, is dependent not on "man whose breath is in his nostrils"[9]; it is dependent only on our realization and recognition of the indwelling Christ and our ability to receive Its impartations, to hear the "still small voice."[10]

Daily Practice
Establishes Peace

If you will make a practice daily of realizing "where I am, God is; the place whereon I stand is holy ground[11]; God in the midst of me is mighty,[12] and all they that are opposed, they have but the arm of flesh, or nothingness; we have the Lord God Almighty[13]; the Lord God in the midst of me is mighty, and there is no might external to me, not in the mind of man or the matter of man," then you will begin to prove that that which heretofore has been opposition in your life; that which heretofore has been discordant or the source of discord; that which heretofore has been a barrier to your progress, to your prosperity, to your happiness— these will begin to fall away.

And then, you will see that this principle operates. The moment you see this operate in your experience without your telling anyone, someone will be led to you and will say, "Give me help." You won't know why they've picked you, and they won't, because it's an invisible occurrence. The darkness always finds the light, so the darkness can be dispelled. The moment you begin to prove your understanding of this, that there is no power external to you, that God in the midst of you is omnipotence, and there is no power external to you for good or evil in person, thing, or condition; that there is no mental power, no physical power that is power, for all power is given unto you, you will have dominion over everything that appears in your world. And the minute you begin to prove that for one neighbor, one relative, two neighbors, two relatives, you have the sufficient grace to do it for twenty. By this time, you will begin to realize, "Why this is a universal truth!" And you will begin to know it for your community, your elections, your weather, and the events of the world.

Always in secrecy—this is a very sacred thing—and in secrecy, you realize the kingdom of God is within me. Always remember the Master on prayer: Pray secretly and pray sacredly. Never voice your prayer outwardly or openly. And never pray for others to see or to know that you're praying. Make prayer a secret practice and a sacred one. And whatsoever takes place within your consciousness God will bring to bear outwardly. But remember, prayer must be secret; it must be sacred. It must be like a seed buried in the ground where nothing can reach it; nothing can upset it; nothing can harm it. So your prayer is kept in secrecy within you, the prayer of realization: "I and the Father are one,[14] all that the Father hath is mine.[15] Where I am, God is. Where

God is, I am, and therefore, that place whereon I stand is holy ground; all power is given unto me"[16]; all dominion is given unto me. Over what and over whom? Over the belief that there are any external powers. All power is given to me through the understanding that God is Spirit, and spiritual power is the only power.

Just look throughout your human life, and you will see that everything in your life is functioning on the basis of good and evil. There is good one day and evil the next; there is good in this experience and evil in this. Sometimes the things that are good for us today are bad for us tomorrow. The things that may be bad for us today are of no power tomorrow. In other words, we volley back and forth between the two powers of good and evil. But in proportion as this spiritual Son is raised up in us, the Son of God, these laws do not operate anymore. We are not receptive or responsive to them, and not only that, but we aid in nullifying them for others who may come to us. In other words, where there is light, it dispels darkness.

In mystical literature, you have that period of life that is described as going from darkness into light, in dying to mortality and being clothed upon with immortality. That is that period at which we pass from living under the law to living under grace.

Now, in this experience of grace, where immunity is developed to the things of law, you begin to understand that you live in an entirely different world. Now, you don't have to consider the law; you don't have to consider or be concerned, or as the Master said, "take thought for your life"; you don't have to "take thought for your life about what you shall eat or what you shall drink or wherewithal ye shall be clothed"; you don't have to take thought for your life about your future or the latter years. Why? Because having found the kingdom of God, dwelling now in the kingdom of God, there is something else taking responsibility for your entire experience. You learn now "the government is on His shoulder."[17] Whose shoulder? This spiritual Entity or divine Son, which is now raised up in us.

No, "My kingdom is not of this world,"[18] and I am not seeking any jurisdiction over our government, or your government, or any government in the world. All I want is dominion over my consciousness to the extent that every day, I want at least one meditation period, if it's only for three minutes, in which to realize,

Thank you, Father. I am God-governed, God-maintained, God-sustained, and this is the spiritual truth about everyone in our land and on our globe.

In this way, I have dominion. I assert my God-given dominion over my invisible world, and this has the effect of operating in human experience for the universal good.

Peace Within
Becomes Harmony Without

We are yet to become aware of the fact that we embrace our world within ourselves; that all that exists as persons, places, and things live only within our consciousness. We could never become aware of anything outside the realm of our minds. All that is within our mental kingdom is joyously and harmoniously directed and sustained by the laws within. We do not direct or enforce these laws; they eternally operate within us and govern the world without. The peace within becomes the harmony without. As our thought takes on the nature of inner freedom, it loses its sense of fear, doubt, or discouragement. As the realization of our dominion dawns in thought, more assurance, confidence, and certainty become evident. We become a new being, and the world reflects back to us our own higher attitude toward it. Gradually, an understanding of our fellow man and his problems unfolds to us from within, and more love flows out from us, more tolerance, cooperativeness, helpfulness, and compassion, and we find the world responds to our newer concept of it, and then all the universe rushes to us to pour its riches and treasures in our lap.

Only what we live in our consciousness becomes our conscious life. Only what we can embody, embrace within our consciousness, can we demonstrate externally. That which we spiritually realize, we externally demonstrate. The kingdom of God within becomes the realm of peace and harmony and joy without.

Therefore, what we entertain in consciousness is what we demonstrate in life—no more, no less. That is why the Master gave us this: "As ye sow so shall ye reap."[19] And if you sow five minutes of God a day, you'll reap five minutes of God. If you sow "praying without ceasing,"[20] you'll reap praying without ceasing. It is the sowing that you do that brings about the reaping. "If you sow to the flesh, you reap corruption."[21]

Now, theologically, that has been misinterpreted and mistaught so that people believe that sowing to the flesh means "if you commit physical sins." It hasn't any such meaning at all. It means that if you put power out here in effect, that is what you're going to sow—some good and some bad. If you sow to the Spirit, which means if you consciously realize that Spirit is your life, Spirit is your law, Spirit is your government, that's what you're going to sow—spiritual harmony. It's like all phases of life. What we put into it is what we get out of it. What we put into our study, what we put into our practice, what we put into our devotion, what we put into living The Infinite Way—that's what comes back, because here it is: "As ye sow so shall ye reap."

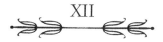

TRUTH TAKES OVER YOUR LIFE

G LORIFY THE CREATOR of all forms, whether it's thought-form or thing-form, and then you'll have neither good nor evil, neither good power nor evil power. You'll have only God-power. And then you'll find one day that for a brief second, you'll be right back in the Garden of Eden where there isn't a problem, where there isn't a force or a power acting on you for either good or evil. You're suspended in an atmosphere of peace.

That's our natural estate, and that's the one to which we must all return, in which we are in a natural state of peace with no good powers to help us, no bad powers to harm us, but God's power always maintaining and sustaining Its image and likeness, and God-power recognized as "I in the midst of you."[1]

"I in the midst of you" maintains you and sustains you. "I do not give my power to another,"[2] says God. "*I* do not give my power to thoughts or things; *I* alone am power." God alone is power. "*I* don't impart that power to thoughts or things. *I* am the power in the midst of you; surrender yourselves to Me."

Give yourselves up and let the *I* at the center of your being be the all-power and the only power, and look out at everything in life and everybody in life and say, "Thou

191

couldest have no power over me unless it came from the
Father within me."3

Herein lies the essence of biblical wisdom: Cut off from
the vine, the branch withers, no longer having access to the
Source; cut off from the Father's house, or Consciousness,
the prodigal consorts with the swine; cut off from their
Source and expelled from the garden of Eden, Adam and
Eve are compelled to live on their substance. In all three
illustrations, there is the one spiritual lesson: When we are
cut off from the Source of our being, we are using up our
life—our mind, strength, health, wisdom, guidance, and
direction, and eventually we come to that period when we
are withered.

On the other hand, by maintaining our contact with the
vine, by maintaining our relationship with the Father as the
Son or heir, or by remaining in Eden, in the kingdom of
God, we draw on the infinite storehouse. This way leads to
eternality, immortality, infinity, harmony, completeness, and
perfection. As human beings living a materialistic life in the
world, we are the branch that is cut off from the tree; we are
the prodigal without a father; we are Adam expelled from
the garden. Living such a life, there is no God-government,
God-protection, or God-sustenance.

When I use my mind to become aware of truth, to know
the truth, to realize the truth, that truth becomes the law
of harmony unto my experience. The truth that I entertain
in my consciousness takes over my life. It eliminates the
discords and inharmony; it brings about peace, harmony,
and security.

You know now what your goal in life is: to be reunited
with the Father, consciously one with God. You know the

way: the prayer of inner contemplation, meditation, the recognition of the Christ, the love of God, the love of man.

O, my child! The blessing that is yours as *My* peace descends upon you, and envelops and sustains you!

Wisdoms of *The Infinite Way*

God-Given Dominion

Your dominion is over your consciousness of government, your awareness of government, your choice of government; therefore, you're not choosing who shall govern "me." You are merely choosing how you shall be governed. Then, as a miracle will reveal to you, no matter who is elected, you will find yourself free, or at least freer of intolerable conditions than you have ever been before.

We have dominion over what kind of government we will have. But you can't have that dominion by going outside and deciding who you want to elect and then forcing their election for the simple reason that after they're elected, they may not prove to be the right one. Politicians don't always live up to the promise of their campaigns.

But we will assert our God-given dominion by realizing, "I don't want any man to govern; I want to realize God's government on earth as it is in heaven; I want to realize God's dominion on earth," and cling to that in your daily meditation period for world work, government work, and national work.

Hold to that—that you're not choosing this candidate or that; you're not determining which one is going to do the best, and so forth. You are going to have God-government. You are going to realize God's government. Then, if you do hold to this, you will discover that those most representative of good government will be the ones elected. It may not be one entire party, but it can be the best of two parties or three parties so that eventually, your fate isn't in the hands of a party, and your fate isn't in the hands of certain men.

You continue to realize, "I must be God-governed. I recognize and realize only God's government on earth, even God's government of men." Then, you'll witness not only a different type of person getting into government, but you'll find that those who get in come more or less under the government of a wisdom higher than their own, even though at times they don't know why.

Someday, when we can behold the Christ in our presidents, in our congressmen, and the dictators of the world, instead of seeing them as they appear to be, we will heal the world, nationally and internationally. You probably think that that is easy. But it isn't! And that is the cause of discord and inharmony within ourselves; that is why this path is not an easy one. It demands that we persist until the day comes when we look right into the soul of those we consider the most wicked and behold the incarnation of God. When there are those capable of this, there will be permanent peace on earth.

Many of you have read in our writings the quoted statement that "You can talk about water forever, but it will not quench your thirst. You must drink." You have heard it said over again and over, that talking about meals and banquets will not satisfy you. You must eat. And we say to you that you can talk about God, and you can read about God, and you can praise God, and you can worship God from now to eternity, and never experience a single moment of harmony or peace. Talking about God, reading about God, is just about as fruitful as talking about meat and talking about water, or reading about them. It isn't tasting; it isn't drinking; it isn't eating!

For many, many years, I have said that the day would come when we would stop talking truth and would feel it, would live it, would experience it. From the first shovelful of dirt that is carried away, progress is being made in leveling the entire mountain. But a mountain is made up of countless shovelfuls of earth and stone, and not until many of these have been removed is it apparent that any noticeable progress has been made.

So it is that when we are aware of the density of human selfhood, we know that we are moving a mountain of ignorance. Although a beginning is made with our first serious meditation, progress will not be too evident for a long, long time. Then all of a sudden, it seems to burst upon us like a flash of light.

When we have been touched by the Spirit, it is evident in the light shining forth from our eyes and the glow on our face. Outwardly our life changes. Our human relationships change, our nature changes, and our health changes. Sometimes, even our physical form changes, but only because such changes are the outer manifestation of an inner glory, an inner light, which has been attained by contact with the Father within and which has once again established us in Eden.

Our purpose is to be the transparency through which the Light—not we, but the Light—performs Its mighty works, to be the instrument through which the Divine can manifest and express Itself on earth as It does in heaven.

We are never the doer; we are never the actor. We are always the vacuum through which Spirit flows. Let us never for a moment believe that by our spiritual endowments, we will ever attain personal or spiritual power. There is no room in spiritual living for egotism or the exercise of personal power. God does not give His power to another. God does not give His glory to another. The power, the glory, and the dominion always remain in God, and we are but instruments, humble servants, or transparencies through which that Light may shine.

The Peace of Eden Rests Within Me

In the beginning in the Edenic days, man was complete, whole, and harmonious—one with God. By the grace of God, everything flourished, and there was peace. What man is now striving to attain in his search for God is the reestablishment of that Edenic state of complete peace and harmony, a state in which we are not at war with one another, but in love with one another; a state in which we do not deprive others, but share and give to others.

The hope of man has been that by finding some supernatural power, he would be able to recapture that state of bliss on earth. It must be clear to every thinking person, however, that in his attempt to find harmony, man has been searching in the wrong way and in the wrong place. Individual harmony and world peace will never be established by searching for some supernatural power. Man's need is to reestablish himself in his original Edenic estate, which is oneness with God.

Hundreds of years of frustration and failure should have proved to the world that it is not the work of a God to do this for us. It is our work to do it for ourselves by establishing that original relationship of oneness. The Master said, "Ye shall know the truth and the truth shall make you free."[4] Nowhere does he indicate that this is God's responsibility. Time and time again, he reiterates that it is our responsibility. "Ye shall know the truth… Ye shall love the Lord thy God…[5] Ye shall love thy neighbor as thyself…[6] Ye shall pray for the enemy…[7] Ye shall forgive seventy times seven…[8] Ye shall bring the tithes into the storehouse."[9] In no place and at no time does he place the responsibility for our sense of separation from God upon God, but upon us. To us is addressed the entire teaching of Jesus Christ—not to God, to us.

You know what the goal of life is—to be reunited with the Father, to be consciously one with God. You know the way—the prayer of inner contemplation and meditation, the recognition of the Christ, the love of God, and the love of man. Now carry this message in your mind where you will always remember the principles, and in your heart, dwell upon the gift which has been given you, delivered to you from the Father—the gift of the realized Presence within you. Bless It always that It may increase.

When you pray, pray that God's grace be active in the consciousness of mankind. Do not make the mistake made in the religious world, that of praying for God to improve the human being or the human world. Pray that the Son of God be revealed in individual man; pray that the Son of God be raised up in individual man; pray that God's government reign on earth.

For a period of five or ten or fifteen years, it is possible to have good government on earth, but it is never permanent. Why? Because it is not given to man's wisdom to govern impartially and with wisdom. Therefore, unless you are praying that God's government be revealed on earth, you are praying amiss. Remember this: Whether our administration is Republican or whether it is Democratic, exchanging one set of men for another set of men will not solve the problems of this world. When men are inspired by God, they govern well, and it makes no difference who they are or what political party they belong to. When men govern by personal interest, they govern poorly or, if well, temporarily.

The change that must come about from this period on is this: In your innermost heart, your prayer must be that the kingdom of God be established in the hearts and souls of men; that God's government rule the consciousness of mankind; that all men subject themselves unto the wisdom and the will of God. If you and I cannot meet this requirement in our individual lives, do not try to pray this way for the world.

First of all, place yourself in subjection to God. Pray that your soul and mind and body be subject unto God. Pray that the will of God be established in you. Remember to repeat this reminder within yourself many times a day.

Let Thy will be done in me. Let Thy wisdom rule me. Let Thy love flow through me that I may be wise, loving, benevolent, just.

This is somewhat like Solomon's prayer when he took over his high office, that he be given God's wisdom. As you surrender yourself to God's government, to the reign of God, to the spiritual center of man that man may be spiritually-inspired and God-endowed, you are in some measure dealing more wisely, kindly, lovingly, benevolently, and more justly with your neighbor—and more forgivingly with your enemy.

And if I wish to be God-governed, I must be still. I must be still and let God's government take over. Yes, there are certain things I must do to prepare myself for God's government. I've learned this from the Master: not to expect God's government if I'm holding somebody in desire for revenge. If I'm holding somebody in hate, there's no way for God to break through my consciousness. The reason is— this comes to you at this stage of unfoldment—that God is love. But God is not a love out here that comes to me. God is a love that I let flow out from me. But since love means forgiveness, benevolence, cooperation, mutuality, sharing, giving, there is no love in me unless those qualities are being expressed. Therefore, to fit myself for God's government, which means the government of love, I must make myself an instrument through which love can flow.

And so, step by step, we are strengthened until the day comes when we realize that now we can rest at will in God and let that Spirit that flows through us, that Robe that envelops us, be the prayer, the benediction, and the healing to our community and to the world.

We become the light of the world as we bring ourselves to a state of consciousness in which we do not battle the errors of the world, but in which we become completely still and let the Spirit of God nullify and dissolve the pictures of sense. No longer will we struggle with error, but rest, relax, and bear witness to God functioning on earth as in heaven. Above all, we will never forget that we are the twelve, the seventy, the two hundred. We are the light in our community. We are that one, even if there is not another, who will not succumb to the mesmerism of fear, doubt, hate, envy, jealousy, or malice. We are that one who will be a rock in our community, a rock of Silence, welling up within ourselves as peace, and letting that peace descend upon our community.

A Call for Commitment

CITIZENS OF THE United States have the opportunity and privilege of voting for their choice for the next president of the United States, a privilege they have had for so long that many have taken it lightly and have failed to avail themselves of this opportunity. Let us accept this opportunity as a solemn commitment and enter into it prayerfully, seeking inner guidance and knowing the spiritual identity, not only of the candidates but of every voter, that each one may be an instrument for the divine government.

Let us, in this moment of meditation, realize government by God, government by the activity of the Christ in human consciousness, government administered by the inspired thought of men and women dedicated to the principles on which this nation was founded.

Joel S. Goldsmith

Scriptural References and Notes

AN INVITATION

   1. Matthew 7:14

PART 1
THE COURAGEOUS CHOICE

I. TO BE GOVERNED BY GOD OR GOVERNED BY MAN

   1. Isaiah 9:6

   2. Genesis 18:33

   3. Benjamin Franklin, Speech to the Constitutional Convention (1787)

   4. Victor Hugo

   5. Revelations 21:27

   6. Isaiah 2:22

   7. John 3:16

   8. Isaiah 45:2

   9. John 14:2

   10. Psalms 146:3

   11. John 10:30

   12. Acts 17:28

   13. Colossians 3:3

   14. I Corinthians 2:14

   15. Psalms 118:24

   16. Psalms 127:1

   17. Luke 17:21

   18. Hebrews 12:2

II. THE GENESIS OF IDENTITY

   1. Isaiah 2:22

   2. Deuteronomy 6:4

   3. Mark 12:29

   4. Acts 17:28

   5. Matthew 16:13-15

   13. Matthew 5:44-45

   14. Joshua 24:15

   15. Revelations 21:27

   16. Frederick Douglass

   17. Matthew 18:20

6. Matthew 16:16
7. Mark 1:24
8. Luke 15:31
9. Exodus 3:5
10. Romans 8:8
11. Matthew 5:38
12. Galatians 3:26

18. Genesis 18:32
19. John 14:27
20. Isaiah 9:6
21. John 16:7
22. Romans 8:17
23. Matthew 25:40

PART 2
THE GARDEN OF EDEN

III. HEAVEN IS EARTH SPIRITUALLY UNDERSTOOD

1. John 18:36
2. John 10:30
3. Matthew 4:18-20
4. John 7:24
5. Matthew 19:17
6. I Samuel 3:9
7. John 17:16
8. John 14:9
9. Mark 8:27-29
10. Matthew 19:6
11. I Corinthians 2:14
12. Romans 8:7
13. John 15:5-6
14. Robert Burns, 'Man Was Made to Mourn, A Dirge.', (1784), 55.

15. John 5:30-31
16. John 14:10
17. Mark 10:18
18. Romans 8:9
19. I Kings 19:11-12
20. Romans 8:9, 17
21. John 18:36
22. Matthew 26:52
23. Psalms 121:4
24. Alfred, Lord Tennyson, "The Higher Pantheism", Holy Grail volume (1869) stanza 6.
25. I Thessalonians 5:17
26. Isaiah 9:6

PART 3
INTO A FAR COUNTRY

IV. WHEN WE ARE TEMPTED BY GOOD AND EVIL

1. Genesis 3:11
2. Genesis 2:17
3. John 18:36
4. William Shakespeare, Hamlet, Act II, Scene II, lines 249-250.
5. John 19:11
6. Mark 10:18
7. Romans 7:15-20
8. Luke 23:43
9. John 9:3
10. Matthew 22:39
11. Matthew 7:12
12. Matthew 5:23-24
13. I Corinthians 15:31
14. John 16:33
15. Deuteronomy 6:4
16. Romans 8:7
17. Exodus 14:13
18. I Samuel 17:45
19. Genesis 18:32
20. Galatians 6:7
21. Matthew 7:12
22. Matthew 18:18
23. Galatians 6:8
24. Isaiah 2:20
25. Algernon Charles Swinburne, 'Hertha', The Poetry of Algernon Charles Swinburne - Volume III: Songs Before Sunrise, (London: Chatto & Windus, 1904), line 15.
26. John 10:30
27. John 14:9
28. Joel 2:25
29. Romans 8:8

V. WHEN JUDGING BY APPEARANCES

1. Luke 12:14
2. Genesis 1:31
3. John 15:7-8
4. John 8:32
5. Matthew 23:9
6. I Kings 19:12
7. Matthew 3:17
8. Matthew 14:27
9. John 7:24
10. John 16:33
11. Hebrews 12:2
12. Luke 24:6
13. Isaiah 2:22
14. Matthew 6:33
15. Matthew 18:21-22
16. Luke 23:34

VI. WHEN WE ARE TEMPTED TO ARGUE OR FIGHT: "DON'T FIGHT 5!"

1. John 8:12
2. Mark 8:23-25
3. John 5:8
4. I Corinthians 6:19
5. Matthew 26:52
6. II Corinthians 3:17
7. Psalms 16:11
8. Luke 4:8
9. Matthew 6:4
10. Isaiah 2:22
11. I John 4:4
12. Isaiah 30:15
13. John 17:3
14. Matthew 5:39
15. John 14:27
16. Galatians 5:7
17. John 14:2
18. Matthew 10:36
19. Psalms 46:6
20. Philippians 2:5
21. John 8:32
22. Matthew 7:12
23. Galatians 6:8
24. Psalms 91:1,10
25. John 15:7
26. Isaiah 54:17
27. II Chronicles 20:15-17
28. Matthew 5:25
29. Mary Baker Eddy, Science and Health with Key to the Scriptures (Boston: The Christian Science Publishing Society, 1875), pp. 16-17.
30. Robert Browning, "Pippa's Song", The Oxford Book of English Verse, ed. by Arthur Quiller-Couch, (Oxford: Clarendon Press, 1919), I, lines 7-8.
31. I Thessalonians 5:17

VII. WHEN WE INDULGE IN CONDEMNATION

1. Romans 8:9
2. Luke 23:34
3. Exodus 20:16
4. John 16:15
5. Romans 7:19-20
6. Matthew 25:40
7. Matthew 25:45
8. Galatians 6:7
9. Deuteronomy 5:9
10. Acts 10:34
11. John 8:11
12. John 10:30
13. Romans 13:10
14. Matthew 22:49

VIII. WHEN WE SPREAD FEAR, RUMOR, HYSTERIA, AND MASS CONFUSION

1. Acts 17:28
2. Isaiah 45:22
3. Joshua 24:15
4. Hebrews 13:5
5. Matthew 28:20
6. Matthew 4:18-22
7. Philippians 4:7
8. Philippians 2:5
9. Genesis 18:32
10. Ezekiel 21:27
11. Psalms 91:10
12. Matthew 26:26-28
13. Luke 10:30-37
14. II Chronicles 32:8
15. John 16:15
16. Exodus 3:5
17. John 10:30
18. John 8:11
19. Alfred, Lord Tennyson, "The Higher Pantheism", Holy Grail volume (1869) stanza 6.
20. Psalms 118:6
21. Matthew 5:44-46
22. Luke 6: 32-35
23. Matthew 23:9

IX. WHEN WE PERSONALIZE GOOD AND EVIL

1. Matthew 5:23-24
2. Luke 4:8
3. Luke 23:34
4. John 19:11
5. John 10:30
6. Psalm 91:10
7. Victor Hugo
8. Job 23:14
9. Luke 22:42
10. Galatians 2:20
11. Matthew 6:10
12. Acts 1:24
13. Samuel Butler
14. Matthew 23:9
15. John 20:17
16. Exodus 3:5
17. Hebrews 13:5
18. Matthew 14:27
19. John 14:10
20. II Corinthians 3:17
21. Romans 8:7
22. Romans 8:7-9
23. Psalm 19:12

X. WHEN WE PRAY AMISS

1. John 15:4-8
2. St. Bernard of Clairvaux
3. Matthew 6:25-33
4. Matthew 6:10
5. I Samuel 3:9
6. John 14:10
7. Galatians 2:20
8. Acts 10:34

9. Psalm 46:10
10. Zephaniah 3:17
11. Alfred, Lord Tennyson, "The Higher Pantheism", Holy Grail volume (1869) stanza 6.
12. Isaiah 30:15
13. Psalm 46:6
14. John 5:30-31
15. II Chronicles 32:8

PART 4
RETURN TO THE GARDEN OF EDEN

XI. WHEN PEACE DESCENDS

1. Hebrews 4:9-11
2. Zechariah 4:6
3. Matthew 6:25
4. Romans 8:11, 16
5. Romans 8:17
6. Matthew 10:34
7. II Corinthians 12:9
8. John 14:27
9. Isaiah 2:22
10. I Kings 19:11
11. Exodus 3:5

12. Zephaniah 3:17
13. II Chronicles 32:8
14. John 10:30
15. John 16:15
16. Matthew 28:18
17. Isaiah 9:6
18. John 18:36
19. Galatians 6:7
20. I Thessalonians 5:17
21. Galatians 6:8

XII. THE TRUTH TAKES OVER YOUR LIFE

1. Zephaniah 3:17
2. Isaiah 42:8
3. John 19:11
4. John 8:32
5. Deuteronomy 6:5

6. Mark 12:31
7. Matthew 5:44
8. Matthew 18:21-22
9. Malachi 3:10

Joel S. Goldsmith
Source Material Corresponding
to the Chapters of This Book

Many of Joel Goldsmith's books, including this one, are based on his recorded classwork, which has been preserved in both audio file format and written transcripts. The listing below shows the source material related to each chapter of this book, in the order in which it appears, including published books and previously unpublished transcripts.

Books listed are available at www.acropolisbooks.com

Transcripts listed are available at www.joelgoldsmith.com

AN INVITATION

A Parenthesis in Eternity: Chapter 2, Release God

Living Now: Chapter 1, Living Now

PART 1
THE COURAGEOUS CHOICE

I. TO BE GOVERNED BY GOD OR GOVERNED BY MAN

I Stand on Holy Ground: Chapter 11, Self-Purification, The Way to Mystical Consciousness

Transcript 164A: 1956 Seattle Closed Class, Seeking and Recognizing Your Teacher and Teaching

Transcript 168A: 1956 Portland Open Class, Know the Nature of God – Be Above the Law

Living Now: Chapter 10, An Idea Whose Time Has Come

Transcript 534A: 1963 New York Special Class, Our Spiritual Goal; Comments on Dallas

Transcript 438B: 1961 Hawaiian Village Open Class, Freedom Spiritually Discerned

A Parenthesis in Eternity: Chapter 2, Release God

Transcript 564B: 1964 London Special Class, Consciousness of the Presence of God Is the Freedom

Living Now: Chapter 1, Living Now

Transcript 320A: 1960 Indianapolis Special Class, Conscious Experience of God

A Parenthesis in Eternity: Chapter 3, The Spiritual Adventure

Transcript 455A: 1962 San Diego Special Class, The Principles of Contemplative Meditation

The Altitude of Prayer: Chapter 10, The Widening Circle of Prayer

The Foundation of Mysticism: Chapter 6, One Power

Transcript 13A: 1952 Honolulu Class Series One, Judging by Appearances, The Theatre

Transcript 704B: 1955 Johannesburg Closed Class, Spiritual Breakfast, the Nature of God, Prayer and Meditation, Continued

II. THE GENESIS OF IDENTITY

Living Between Two Worlds: Chapter 1, Opening The Door To Infinity

Transcript 204B: Contemplative Meditation: God as No Power, Part 2

Conscious Union with God: Chapter 5, The Nature of Error

Living Between Two Worlds: Chapter 8, The Way to Fulfillment: Right Identification

Transcript 84A: 1954 Honolulu Closed Class, Cosmic Law

The Joel Goldsmith Reader: Living the Principle of Impersonalization

The Gift of Love: Chapter 1, Love as Understanding

Transcript 525B: 1963 London Work, Foundation of 1963 Message

Transcript 400A: 1961 San Diego Special Class, The Essence of The Infinite Way, Part 1

Beyond Words & Thoughts: Chapter 12, God Revealing Himself as Christ on Earth

Transcript 7B-1: 1952 New Washington Series, Questions & Answers, Including Supply, Tithing, Giving

A Parenthesis in Eternity: Chapter 6, God, the Consciousness of the Individual

PART 2
THE GARDEN OF EDEN

III. HEAVEN IS EARTH SPIRITUALLY UNDERSTOOD

PART 3
INTO A FAR COUNTRY

The Thunder of Silence: Chapter 16, That Ye May Be the Children of Your Father

The Thunder of Silence: Chapter 4, Who Told You?

V. WHEN WE JUDGE BY APPEARANCES

Transcript 546B: 1964 Oahu/Maui Series, Between Two Worlds - Material Sense, Spiritual Discernment

Transcript 204B: 1958 Adelaide Closed Class, Contemplative Meditation: "God As No Power" Side 2

Transcript 183B: 1957 Chicago Open Class, Spiritual Healing – "World Wide" Interest

The Thunder of Silence: Chapter 8, Henceforth Know We No Man After the Flesh

The Heart of Mysticism, Vol IV: Chapter 8, Your Names Are Written in Heaven

Transcript 434B: 1961 Maui Advanced Work, Attaining "That Mind"

Transcript 166A: 1956 Seattle Closed Class, Neither Good nor Evil

Transcript 496B: 1962 London Special Class, Temple Not Made With Hands

Transcript 562B: 1964 London Studio Class, World Work – We May Not Pass By on the Other Side

Realization of Oneness: Chapter 5, Resting in Oneness

Transcript 551A: 1963 Instructions for Teaching The Infinite Way, The Simplicity of the Healing Work

Transcript 477B: 1962 Princess Kaiulani Open Class, Infinite Way Healing Principles

The Thunder of Silence: Chapter 4, "Who Told You?"

Transcript 68A: 1954 Honolulu Lecture Series, Infinite Way Treatment

Transcript 128A: 1955 Kailua Study Group, Bear Witness to God in Action

Transcript 13A: 1952 Honolulu Class Series One, Judging By Appearances-The Theater

Transcript 204B: 1958 Adelaide Closed Class, Contemplative Meditation: "God As No Power" Side 2

Transcript 187A: 1957 First Halekou Closed Class, Beginning of Wisdom (No Power)

I Stand on Holy Ground: Chapter 11, Self-Purification, the Way to the Mystical Consciousness

Transcript 70B: 1954 Honolulu Lecture Series, Nature of God, Prayer, and Error

The Mystical I: Chapter 8, I Speaks

Transcript 469B: 1962 Chicago Closed Class, Third Stage of Our Unfoldment

VI. WHEN WE ARE TEMPTED TO ARGUE OR FIGHT: "DON'T FIGHT 5!"

Living Now: Chapter 10, An Idea Whose Time Has Come

Transcript 68A: 1954 Honolulu Lecture Series, Infinite Way Treatment

Transcript 494A: 1962 London Special Class, Spiritual Power – Temporal Non-Power

Transcript 551A: 1963 Instructions for Teaching The Infinite Way, The Simplicity of the Healing Work (Class given in 1964)

Transcript 320A: 1960 Indianapolis Special Class, Conscious Experience of God

Transcript 352A: 1960 England Open Class, Transcendental Consciousness - Not By Might Nor By Power

Transcript 323A: 1960 Chicago Open Class, The Way

Practicing the Presence: Chapter 7, Meditation

Transcript 520B: 1963 Kailua Private Class, The New Teaching, Part 2

Transcript 613A: 1951 First Northwest Series, The True and False Sense of "I"

Realization of Oneness: Chapter 8, On the Sea of Spirit

Living Now: Chapter 10, An Idea Whose Time Has Come

Transcript 434B: 1961 Maui Advanced Work, Attaining "That Mind"

Transcript 198B: 1957 Second Halekou Closed Class, The Experience

Transcript 19A: 1952 Honolulu Closed Class, Fulfillment

Transcript 92B: 1954 Northwest Series – Portland, Three Points of Practice

Transcript 704B: 1955 Johannesburg Closed Class, Spiritual Breakfast, the Nature of God, Prayer and Meditation, Continued

Transcript 439B: 1961 Hawaiian Village Open Class, Address the World Silently with Peace

Consciousness Transformed: September 21, 1963, The Adjustment Must be Made Within Your Consciousness-A Lesson in Secrecy

The Contemplative Life: Chapter 11, Supply and Secrecy

Transcript 382A: 1960 Auckland Closed Class, Bringing Forth from Within

Practicing the Presence: Chapter 10, The Vision to Behold

Living Now: Chapter 10, An Idea Whose Time Has Come

Transcript 314B: 1960 Denver Closed Class, Foundation of Our Day

The Altitude of Prayer: Chapter 10, The Widening Circle of Prayer

Transcript 198B: 1957 Second Halekou Closed Class, The Experience

A Parenthesis in Eternity: Chapter 2, Release God

Transcript 1007AB: 1951 Portland Class, Activity of the Christ Individual Consciousness

Transcript 485B: 1962 Maui Special Class, The Christ Ministry of the Still Small Voice

Transcript 1006AB: 1951 Portland Class, My Vision of 1950 of the Blanket of Spirit

I Stand on Holy Ground: Chapter 5, Nothing Takes Place Outside of Consciousness

IX. WHEN WE PERSONALIZE GOOD AND EVIL

Transcript 267B: 1959 Hawaiian Village Closed Class, Self-Purification, Continued

Transcript 379B: 1960 Sydney Closed Class, Answered Prayer

Transcript 309B: 1960 Seattle Closed Class, Coming Into the Awareness of Spirit

*The Altitude of Praye*r: Chapter 10, The Widening Circle of Prayer

Transcript 427A: 1961 New York Special Class, World Affairs Spiritually Handled

Transcript 379B: 1960 Sydney Closed Class, Answered Prayer

Transcript 356B: 1960 England Open Class, Putting Up the Sword Is the Secret

Living the Illumined Life: Chapter 7, Preparation for Spiritual Baptism Transcript

Transcript 106B: 1954 Seattle Closed Class, Infinite Way
Treatment Summarized, Part 2

Transcript 558: 1964 Instructions for Infinite Way Practitioners,
Instructions for Infinite Way Practitioners

The Heart of Mysticism, Vol II: Chapter 12, Christmas 1955

Transcript 500B: 1962 Holland Closed Class, Attuning to
Consciousness

Transcript 267B: 1959 Hawaiian Village Closed Class, Self-
Purification, Continued

Living Now: Chapter 10, An Idea Whose Time Has Come

Transcript 497A: 1962 Stockholm Closed Class, Sowing to the
Spirit – or to the Flesh

Transcript 518A: 1963 Kailua Private Class, Consciously Attaining
the Experience of Oneness

A Parenthesis in Eternity: Chapter 15, Self-Surrender

Transcript 156A: 1956 Chicago Open Class, Start Healing Today

Beyond Words and Thoughts: Chapter 3, Thou Shalt Not Make Unto
Thee Any Graven Image

Transcript 510A: 1963 Instructions for Teaching The Infinite Way,
Do Not Meet a Problem on the Level of the Problem and Other
Points in Healing and Teaching

Transcript 458B: 1962 Los Angeles Center Open Class, The Inner
Kingdom

Transcript 422A: 1961 Lausanne Closed Class, Answered Prayer

X. WHEN WE PRAY AMISS

The Altitude Of Prayer: Chapter 4, This Is Immortality

Transcript 514A: 1963 Princess Kaiulani Sunday Series, Labor,
Sabbath, and Grace

Transcript 422A: 1961 Lausanne Closed Class, Answered Prayer

Transcript 124B: 1955 Kailua Study Group, Reality Experienced

The Heart of Mysticism, Vol IV: Chapter 1, Out of Darkness – Light

Transcript 500B: 1962 Holland Closed Class, Attuning to
Consciousness

The Altitude of Prayer: Chapter 10, The Widening Circle of Prayer

Transcript 544A: 1964 Oahu/Maui Series, Spiritual Attainment
through the Door

PART 4
RETURN TO THE GARDEN OF EDEN

The Thunder of Silence: Chapter 18, Ye Are the Light

Practicing the Presence: Chapter 10, The Vision to Behold

Consciousness Transformed: Prayer of the Righteous Man: God Is

Transcript 469B: 1962 Chicago Closed Class, Third Stage of Our Unfoldment

A CALL FOR COMMITMENT

Showing Forth the Presence of God: Chapter 8, The Spiritual Life

Made in the USA
Columbia, SC
03 September 2020